"The power of prayer is the greatest power of the church. Thank you, Sheila, for reminding us to avail ourselves of the privilege of petition."

Max Lucado, pastor and bestselling author

"In *Praying Women*, Sheila reminds us all that prayer is one of the greatest weapons we have to push back the darkness in our world. This book will challenge you to think about prayer in a new way—one rooted in who God is, not who we are or who we want to be."

Christine Caine, bestselling author and founder of A21 and Propel Women

"I have a tremendous amount of love and respect for Sheila. She has a remarkable ability to connect with others through her struggles, and in doing so, she reminds us that we are not alone. In this book, Sheila shares about the confusion and questions she has wrestled with and the truths about prayer she has learned as a result. I believe these truths have the power to awaken the praying woman inside of you!"

Lisa Bevere, *New York Times* bestselling author
and cofounder of Messenger International

"Sometimes we don't know why or even how to pray. Yet prayer is our lifeline to God Himself. Gratefully, Sheila Walsh helps us make sense of 'How to pray when you don't know what to say.' *Praying Women* will guide you on the greatest journey of your life as you learn to persevere in prayer no matter what. It is one of the best books you can possibly read. I highly recommend it!"

Dr. Jack Graham, senior pastor, Prestonwood Baptist Church

"Martin Luther wrote, 'To be a Christian without prayer is no more possible than to be alive without breathing.' And that's what Sheila reminds us of so beautifully in this book: prayer isn't some stale religious discipline, it's the incredible key to intimacy with our Creator Redeemer. Even without words, the posture of prayer brings us fully into the presence of the One who loves us unconditionally. The One to whom we can run to and rest in during times of trouble."

Lisa Harper, author and Bible teacher

"The greatest thing one can do for God and others is to pray. Sheila Walsh is a mighty woman of prayer, and therefore her book is not only vital for every woman to read but will also change the world, because prayer changes the world."

Jeremiah J. Johnston, Ph.D., president, Christian Thinkers Society

"Before you can see it, you've got to speak it. And before you can speak it, you've got to pray about it. The situation doesn't have the power—a praying woman does!"

Sarah Jakes Roberts, pastor, bestselling author,
and founder of Woman Evolve

"This is an extraordinary read! Sheila speaks right to the heart of the issues that daughters of God experience when it comes to prayer. No matter where you are on your spiritual journey, *Praying Women* will help your prayer life come alive as you seek to know God more intimately and ask Him to do the miraculous."

Julie Clinton, president, Extraordinary Women Ministries

Praying Women

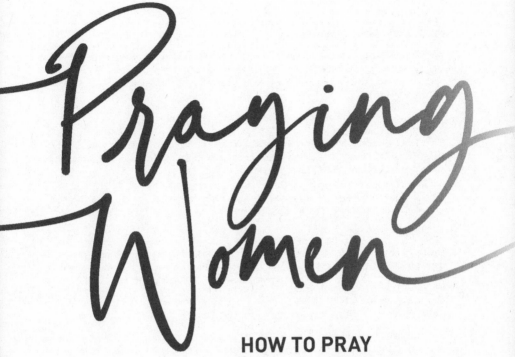

Praying Women

HOW TO PRAY
WHEN YOU DON'T KNOW
WHAT TO SAY

SHEILA WALSH

BakerBooks

a division of Baker Publishing Group
Grand Rapids, Michigan

Published by Baker Books
a division of Baker Publishing Group
PO Box 6287, Grand Rapids, MI 49516-6287
www.bakerbooks.com

Printed in the United States of America

Library of Congress Cataloging-in-Publication Data
Names: Walsh, Sheila, 1956– author.
Title: Praying women : how to pray when you don't know what to say / Sheila Walsh.
Description: Grand Rapids, Michigan : Baker Books, a division of Baker Publishing Group, 2020.
Identifiers: LCCN 2019031918 | ISBN 9780801078026 (cloth)
Subjects: LCSH: Christian women—Religious life. | Prayer—Christianity.
Classification: LCC BV4527 .W3555 2020 | DDC 248.3/2082—dc23
LC record available at https://lccn.loc.gov/2019031918

ISBN 978-0-8010-7803-3 (ITPE)

The author is represented by Dupree Miller and Associates, a global literary agency. www.dupreemiller.com

This book is dedicated with love to
my friend Jennalee Trammel,
a woman who understands the pain
of life and the power of prayer.

Contents

Introduction

> I pray because I can't help myself. I pray because I'm helpless. I pray because the need flows out of me all the time, waking and sleeping. It doesn't change God. It changes me.
>
> C. S. Lewis

Prayer started to confuse me when I was about six years old, all because of a story my mom told me about my grandfather.

My Scottish grandfather was a man of few words. For him, there was one and only one way to do most things. And when it came to prayer before meals, he knew the formula, and it was very simple, stated with a strong, solemn, imagine-he's-a-character-in-the-movie-Braveheart accent: "For what we are about to receive, may the Lord make us trrrruuuuly thankful. Amen."

The end. That was how you did it. That was *the* way to pray.

But one day my dear nana asked my grandfather if he might consider a little expansion to his lifelong standard prayer. It was an important day for the family, and she wanted his prayer to reflect that. As you might imagine, it didn't go well.

Missionaries from Africa were coming to the house for a meal after speaking at church, and Nana had pulled out all the stops for the guests of honor. The wedding china, the family silver, and a Waterford crystal vase filled with pale pink roses from her garden set the stage. Everything was fresh and new . . . apart from one thing: my grandfather.

"William, everything is perfect for our special guests. Before we eat, do you think you could please pray something a wee bit deeper, something bigger, something . . . longer? I want this visit to be perfect."

He grunted loudly, and that was it. It was impossible to tell if it was a grunt of affirmation or not. Only time would tell.

After the guests arrived and sat down at the table, the time had come. This was my grandfather's big moment.

He cleared his throat and bowed his head. There was a pregnant pause. Then this: "For what we are about to receive . . ." The same old line he offered every day, at which point my nana gave him a gentle, okay . . . a big kick under the table. There was an obvious, now uncomfortable, pause. Then the big finale.

"May the Lord make us trrrruuuuly thankful and . . . and . . . and . . . make me a good boy!"

Mum told me she laughed so hard she fell off her seat. Nana, she said, made a noise reminiscent of someone sitting on bagpipes. My grandfather, on the other hand, was not amused. He'd been forced to depart from his usual formula, and it had been all downhill from there.

After hearing that story as a child, I became very worried about this whole prayer thing. What if I was asked to pray in front of people and forgot my lines? There was clearly a right way to do this and a wrong way. What if I got it wrong?

I've thought about that story many times as an adult and smiled at the childlike ending my grandfather tagged onto his grace. What he'd done was combine the two prayers he knew, the family grace and the bedtime prayer he prayed every night as a child, which goes something like this:

Thank you for this day,
watch over me this night,
make me a good boy,
for Jesus's sake. Amen.

I understand my grandfather's panic. Prayer can be intimidating, particularly praying out loud in front of strangers. Throw in the request for an ad-lib and who knows what might go wrong.

My bedtime prayer as a child was this:

Jesus, gentle Shepherd, hear me.
Bless thy little lamb tonight.
Through the darkness be thou near me.
Keep me safe 'til morning light.

As I lay under a picture depicting Christ holding a lamb, I was never quite sure if I was praying for the baby sheep or for me, but I prayed the prayer faithfully every night.

I'd love to say that in the years that followed I became a great prayer warrior, but that's not true. I often struggled to know how to pray and what to pray. If God had already decided what was going to happen, what difference did my prayers really make?

That's not the only problem though, is it? If we're brutally honest, at times we find prayer boring or repetitive. We get distracted, and our minds wander. We know how important prayer is, but we struggle to pray, and then we feel guilty and wonder what's wrong with us. Sometimes this makes us question our commitment to God. Even deeper, does God hear and answer our prayers?

Before starting to write this book, I conducted a quick poll on my Facebook page, asking my readers about their experiences with prayer. Within two hours, there were over 650 comments, many expressing the same struggles.

I get distracted.

I feel like I'm just saying the same things over and over.

What's the point if God knows what's going to happen anyway?

How do I know what I'm supposed to pray?

I get bored.

How do I know God hears me?

I didn't get an answer last time, so why pray?

I feel as if God hates me!

I'm too depressed to pray.

This comment showed up over and over and over:

I can't stay focused; my mind wanders.

I understand. More importantly, so does God. There have been many dark seasons in my life when I found it difficult to pray. That's why I wrote this book. After years of trying to be perfect, I began to understand that God doesn't seek our perfection. He longs for our presence. I've written many books over the years, but I don't think any have impacted me personally as much as this one.

There is so much I'm excited to share with you. The Holy Spirit wants to teach us how to pray and also show us that it's not as complicated as we've made it. I also believe we have an enemy who will do whatever he can to distract us and stop us from praying. If we have forgotten the power of prayer, he has not, but we are not alone!

And the Holy Spirit helps us in our weakness. For example, we don't know what God wants us to pray for. But the Holy Spirit prays for us with groanings that cannot be expressed in words. And the Father who knows all hearts knows what the Spirit is saying, for the Spirit pleads for us believers in harmony with God's own will. (Rom. 8:26–27)

That is amazing news!

I am very grateful you picked up this book. Even now I'm pausing to pray for you. I'm asking the Holy Spirit to open your eyes to see truth and your ears to hear His voice. If you've been tempted to give up on prayer, just know that you're not alone. It doesn't mean you don't love Jesus. It may simply mean that, like my grandfather, you think there's a right way to pray and a wrong way. Or perhaps you're tired of saying the same things over and over again. Maybe you prayed and God didn't answer you, so you think, *Why keep praying?*

Whatever your challenge is, let me remind you that God is not looking for perfect words or perfect people. He just wants our hearts. So together we'll look at how to pray when we don't know what to say, how to pray through our pain, how to pray God's promises over our lives, how to pray when we need a breakthrough, and perhaps most life changing of all, how to pray God's Word back to Him. This one practice alone is changing my life.

May I pray for you?

Father,

I pray right now for the one reading these words. If she is tired, give her rest. If she is broken, bring Your healing. If she is heartsick, bring Your peace. If she feels condemned, bring Your grace. We want to be praying women for Jesus's sake. In His name I ask these things. Amen.

ONE

Pray When You Don't Know What to Say

*Praying women know it's okay
to start where they are.*

In prayer it is better to have a heart without words than words without a heart.

John Bunyan

When you pray, don't babble on and on as the Gentiles do.

Matthew 6:7

One day I would love to be the kind of writer who tucks herself away in a little cottage by the ocean for a few months and writes at leisure between cups of Earl Grey tea and walks on the beach at sunset with her well-behaved dogs. For now, I'm grateful when I have a couple quiet days of uninterrupted writing at home. I never learned to type in school, so I type all my books with two fingers. If you ever find yourself beside me in a coffee shop, you'll move. Even if you think you like me, you'll move. When

I get on a roll, my typing sounds like a demented woodpecker. Me writing at home seems to work best for the rest of the planet.

On this particular day, the dogs were sleeping, and Barry was doing the laundry, so I sat down at my desk in the den, opened my laptop, and looked for the folder I'd recently saved. I typed in "Praying Women," and nothing came up! *That's strange*, I thought. I tried "Women Who Pray," and still nothing. I simplified and typed "Prayer," and all I found was a piece I'd written last year for a magazine. Where was my file? How could pages and pages of hard work just disappear? Isn't everything supposed to be tucked up safely in that Cloud thingy in the sky?

I had been doing research for this book for two years in the middle of a busy travel and television schedule, and now the deadline for the finished manuscript was fast approaching. I'd spent months on airplanes and downtime in hotels reading, praying, and writing notes on yellow legal pads. I'd studied passages of Scripture that teach on prayer and knew what I believed each chapter should hold. During an eight-hour layover in an airport a couple of weeks previously, I'd gathered up all the notes I'd written over the months and finally typed everything into one document, which I saved under . . . under what? When I opened my laptop and typed in "Praying Women" and nothing came up, I panicked. How could it just disappear? I sat back in my chair and took a deep breath. I didn't know what to say. The loss felt overwhelming. Then out of my mouth came one word. I cried out one name: "Jesus!"

My simple prayer at that moment was one word: "Jesus!"

I lifted my hands toward heaven and said His name again. "Jesus!"

Some people use that name casually or even as a curse word, but for me, it is the name I call on in the best of times and the worst of times, when life is falling apart and when it's falling into place. I didn't have many fancy words that day. Just one. His name. One name connecting me to the source of peace.

My husband, Barry, had been in the laundry room, and when he heard me cry out, he ran into the den to see if I'd been raptured.

"Are you okay?" he asked.

"I'm good," I said, nodding my head and smiling.

When you lose everything you've written on prayer, what do you do? Pray!

I finally found my folder saved under a different name, but the Holy Spirit taught me a lesson that day in those few moments of panic: prayer should be my first response in everything. As Corrie Ten Boom once said, "Is prayer your spare tire or your steering wheel?"[1] In other words, is prayer the thing that guides you through every moment in life or something you turn to only in an emergency?

I don't know what you're facing right now. You might be in a very difficult place and praying feels too hard, but do you know that one of the most powerful prayers you can pray is just one word, the name of Jesus?

Anywhere.

Any time.

Any place.

Any situation.

When you have a relationship with Jesus, prayer isn't something you *do*; it's who you *are*.

I simply want you to know that if you have struggled or do struggle with prayer, I have too. I've made commitments to get up early and pray for an hour and fallen asleep on the floor halfway through. I've prayed to lose weight and gained five pounds. I've prayed in great faith for someone to be healed and wept bitter tears at their funeral. I've prayed "according to Your will" and been reprimanded by others who said I was praying with a lack of faith.

We have made prayer far too complicated. Prayer is simply talking with and listening to the One who is crazy in love with you. If you live to be one hundred, you will never meet anyone who loves you the way Jesus does. If you had the best dad in the world, he can't hold a candle to your Father in heaven, who longs to hear from you. Your longing invites His presence.

Because prayer is so central to faith, we think we're supposed to know what we're doing, and because of that, we're often afraid to ask questions. But we all have them. Growing up in Scotland, I know I did. It just took one person's raw, honest prayer to break us all open.

Raw and Real

In retrospect, I realize that to threaten to punch someone at a prayer meeting is not technically in line with Scripture, but at the time, the temptation was almost too much to bear. It was Sunday evening, and the fourteen members of our youth group had gathered in the lower hall of our small Baptist church for our weekly meeting. We sat in a circle on the wooden floor, and after a few choruses accompanied by a slightly out-of-tune guitar, our youth leader suggested that we turn to prayer. He said he would start and invited anyone who wanted to pray to participate. He reminded us that there was no pressure to pray, but after he prayed, the one to his left prayed, then the next, then the next. Like dominoes, we each fell in turn. Most were short prayers, and one was so long that it was hard not to succumb to a nap, but judging by the gentle snores two people down, someone already had. When my turn came, as far as I remember, I thanked God for loving me, for my friends, and for the fact that we had just experienced three days in a row without rain. (The west coast of Scotland is well moisturized.) After my "amen," there was a pause. Sitting to my left was "Bobbie." He hadn't been coming to our church very long, and everything about Christianity and faith was fairly new to him. I was about to whisper to him that he didn't have to pray when he dove right in.

"Jesus. Thanks very much for everything. Thanks for your blood that washes whiter than Tide or Persil. Over and out . . . amen."

There was a pregnant pause, and then one of the boys in our group burst out laughing.

"You can't talk to God like that!" he said. "He's not your pal!"

Bobbie turned bright red, at which point I stood up and was about to punch the other guy in the mouth when our youth leader told me to sit down and behave like a Christian.

"I think that was the best prayer of the night," I said through tears. "Jesus is your friend, Bobbie, and His blood does have remarkable cleaning powers!"

My best friend slid over to where I was sitting in the circle and handed me her handkerchief.

"Why don't we have a few moments of silent prayer," someone suggested, and we all settled down. The rest of that evening opened up into a real, honest, no-question-will-be-judged conversation about prayer. Everything poured out.

Is there a right way to pray?

Are there right words that we should use?

Should we kneel?

Do we have to close our eyes?

How do we know what to pray for?

If God doesn't answer, is it because He's mad at us?

Can we ask for anything, or does it have to be something holy?

Why does God answer some prayers and not others?

Does God have favorites?

Does God ever talk back?

I Stink at Prayer!

The discussion we had that night stayed with me for a long time. I'd wondered about all those things too. I was sixteen years old and passionate about Jesus, but my passion was more about talking to other people *about* Jesus than actually talking *to* Jesus myself. I thought I really stunk at prayer. Have you ever felt like that? Perhaps you listened to someone else pray and it sounded so "right," so holy, and you knew you couldn't come up with anything close to it, so you didn't pray at all. I understand that. I wanted so much to say the right things, ask for the right things, but I wasn't sure what those were. Every time I prayed I said the same things over and over, and I was convinced that God was bored with me, was disappointed with my prayers. Perhaps if I told other people about Him, then He'd be pleased with me. My commitment to talk to others, however, bordered at times on my becoming an absolute public nuisance.

I remember being on a bus heading into town one evening when an unsuspecting man sat down beside me. Smoking was allowed on public transportation back then, and he pulled out a packet of cigarettes. Unable to find his lighter, he turned to me and asked if I had a light. *What an opening line*, I thought as a light bulb brighter than the entire Vegas strip went off in my head. Here was proof that God talks back and answers prayer. I'd prayed that very morning for an opportunity to share my faith, and I already had a potential convert. Turning to face him and in my most sincere and, I hoped, compelling voice, I replied, "Yes! I have the Light of the World." He moved.

At that point in my life, I equated prayer with results. If I saw no results, I imagined either God didn't hear my prayer or He thought it was a bit wonky, like my grandfather's "Make me a good boy" prayer. Think back to your first prayers. Do you remember if you prayed as a child? Perhaps you weren't raised in a praying home. Or you may have been raised in a tradition in which prayers were written down and recited and the idea of crying out to God in a raw, real way when you find yourself in a tough place feels strange or wrong. Perhaps you prayed hard for something and God didn't answer, so you wonder, *Why bother?* My earliest memories of prayer from my childhood fall into one of two categories: one, the prayer Mum taught my sister and me to say each night, and two, the strange prayers Mum would pray when we were in a difficult place.

After my father's death, we lived in government housing. Because we had a very limited income, my sister, my brother, and I were given free school meals, but we still had to have the correct school uniform. At the beginning of a particular new term, my brother hit a growth spurt. His pants were too short, and Mum had no extra money that month. So after supper, she asked us all to gather round her chair as she explained that we were going to ask God for school pants for my brother. I was fascinated by the idea. Do angels wear long pants? Does God keep spares in heaven? After she said, "Amen," I sat there for a while wondering if they would come down the chimney, but nothing happened. A few days later, a friend came to our house for tea with my mum, and when she left, she put a parcel on the sofa. In it were three pairs of long pants in my brother's size. I asked Mum if she'd told her friend of our need, and she reminded me, "No, we told the Lord." She didn't use fancy words or holy language; she just said what we needed. She wasn't surprised by God's answer, but you could have knocked me over with a feather.

This was new information. I could pray and ask God for anything I wanted and He would have it delivered. As you might imagine, things didn't work out quite like that. Davy Jones from the pop group the Monkees didn't show up on my doorstep vowing never-ending love, but I got over it.

Right now, I want you to know one simple truth: God hears your prayers. He loves you and wants a relationship with you, and we build relationships by talking and listening. If you are in a hard place at the moment, remember that when you don't have the words to say, when you're struggling to communicate what's on your heart, there is power in the name of Jesus. (And you don't stink at prayer!)

Just Start Talking

I received a message on my Facebook page from a young woman who said she loved Jesus but couldn't stand being around Christians. She wrote that she felt more judged in her small group at church than anywhere else. Someone had corrected her on a theological inaccuracy in her prayer, and she was devastated. She wanted to walk away, close down, and stop praying.

That made me very sad. The enemy of our souls wants to bring as much division to the body of Christ as possible. If you are young in your faith and you're shut down by another believer, the temptation is to discount everything you've believed to be true. If you've ever experienced that kind of pain, it can be devastating. I remember well.

When I went to seminary at nineteen, it was my first encounter with Christians from every denomination and almost every nation around the world. I was excited to be on a campus with hundreds of believers, as there were very few of us in my little town in Scotland. As well as my classes, I signed up for every prayer group offered on the notice board in the student common room. We prayed for Africa, for India, for single mothers, for the queen, for fellow students. You name it, we prayed for it.

Most of the guys in my classes were kind and friendly. It was some of the women who struggled with me at first. I was one of the youngest female students. Many were in their thirties and, I learned, didn't approve of the way I dressed. Now, before your mind conjures up images of a flirty dresser, I was the antithesis of that. I've always been very modest. In fact, if someone had invented turtle-neck bathing suits, I would have bought stock. But I did like boots and bright colors, and those apparently fell short of their godly norm. I was walking across campus one afternoon in my bright red boots when I saw a group of female students gathered in what was clearly a prayer circle on the grass. I was excited to join them, but as I got close, I heard my name.

Lord Jesus,

We pray right now for Sheila Walsh that she will see the error of her ways and start dressing like a young Christian woman and not like a Jezebel.

I was horrified realizing that was how they saw me. All I knew about Jezebel was that she threatened to kill the prophet Elijah. I had no idea what she wore! I was a shy teenager. I'd never even had a boyfriend. My father's rage and ultimately his suicide had shattered my trust in men. But I thought I'd be safe in seminary, where people had a common commitment to Jesus, particularly among the women. I was devastated. I ran back to my dorm room and threw myself down on my bed, sobbing from a deeply broken place. I felt ashamed. Every negative thing I'd ever thought about myself came rushing back, louder now, more convincing because these women had talked to God about me behind my back.

I decided to talk to the head of the seminary and tell him I had to leave. I clearly did not belong. Dr. Kirby's secretary set up an appointment for the following day. Gilbert Kirby is home with Jesus now, but he was one of God's greatest gifts to me. I knocked gently on his office door, and he invited me in. He listened to everything that poured out of me, then spoke about the love and grace of God that invite us to come as we are. He asked me to stay in college, to forgive the "praying women," and to show up every day and be myself. He was the first person to direct me to a psalm that has been a source of comfort and strength ever since.

> I prayed to the LORD, and he answered me.
>> He freed me from all my fears.
> Those who look to him for help will be radiant with joy;
>> no shadow of shame will darken their faces.
> In my desperation I prayed, and the LORD listened;
>> he saved me from all my troubles.
> For the angel of the LORD is a guard;
>> he surrounds and defends all who fear him.
> Taste and see that the LORD is good.
>> Oh, the joys of those who take refuge in him! . . .
> The LORD hears his people when they call to him for help.
>> He rescues them from all their troubles.
> The LORD is close to the brokenhearted;
>> he rescues those whose spirits are crushed. (Ps. 34:4–8, 17–18)

I went back to my dorm room and underlined these verses in my Bible. I put a star beside this one: "I prayed, and the LORD listened." The idea was so simple. It sounded too good to be true. I wondered if it was particularly true for David, as he was God's anointed one, the one who would go on to become king, or if it was a promise for all of us. It's clear to me now that we can read the Bible, we can study the Bible, but if we don't know how to apply the power of the living Word of God to ourselves, we remain unchanged. As the words of this psalm washed over me, I could feel the shame begin to melt. I had been in church all my life, but I had never fully understood how personal God's love is, how He speaks through His Word right now in the middle of whatever we are facing.

I persevered in seminary, taking Dr. Kirby's kind words to heart. I think I may have taken the part about being myself a tad too literally.

It became clear in my second year that sometimes prayer is nothing more than a carefully crafted piece of prose designed to impress others. The residential students lunched each day in the seminary dining room. It was quite a formal affair, and all the professors sat fully robed at the head table. Each Friday a student would be chosen to say grace. Some may have thought they were being graded on their prayers. Let me give you just a taste. Please forgive me if this sounds a little irreverent, but some days the food was cold before grace was over.

> *Dear God of Abraham, Isaac, and Jacob,*
>
> *I come before Thee now with a heart full of praise, yet restless too. Indeed, as Augustine said, "Our hearts are restless until they rest in Thee." The children of Israel wandered yay nigh these forty years in the wilderness, yet from Thy bountiful resources Thou didst feed them as Thou dost feed us. And now, God of Moses, Elijah, and all the minor prophets, today Thou hast spread a feast before us. . . .*

It was a lot longer, but you get the picture. Well, one Friday after weeks of graces that could have given Augustine's *Confessions* a run for its money, I was asked, with no warning, to give the blessing. I stood up and said:

> *Round my teeth and round my gums,*
> *look out tummy, here it comes!*
> *Thank you, Lord. Amen.*

If silence can be full of horror, the atmosphere in the dining room that day was pregnant with disdain. What broke the silence was Gilbert laughing out loud.

"Short and to the point!" he said as we all enjoyed a hot lunch.

We all have stories. You and I could sit down and talk for hours about our experiences, the good, the bad, and the downright ugly, but my advice is this: don't worry about getting your words right or wrong. Just start. Just start talking. God is listening.

He Is Listening

For two years, I have felt such a strong call to prayer. I wake up in the morning and it's with me, and not as a "You should pray more!" voice of condemnation; it's more like an excitement bubbling up inside me that God is on the move and He's calling His daughters to be part of what He is about to do. That's why I wrote this book, not to make you feel guilty about how much you pray or don't pray but to say that there is a God in heaven, He loves you, and He is listening. Prayer activates the power of God.

I'm praying for you right now and asking God to teach us all the power of prayer in a fresh, new way. Prayer is often the weapon that sits in the closet, stuffed into the back with the old Christmas ornaments. We mean to get to it someday, but someday never comes, and prayer is too important for that. There is nothing that Satan, our enemy, would love more than for us to stop praying or never start. Over the first thirty years of my life, I prayed long prayers and short prayers, but the turning point for me in regard to prayer was when I had no words left.

When I was hospitalized with severe clinical depression in 1992, all my words were gone. The young girl in me who had decided to follow Jesus at eleven years of age was bitterly disappointed in who I had become. I'd promised to be perfect, to never disappoint God, and here I was, on my face on the floor, empty. The only words I silently prayed were these: "Help me."

They didn't sound like a prayer to me. I heard them as words of total defeat. They were the sounds of a drowning woman, but I believe God heard them as honest words of surrender. For the first time in my life, I admitted to God and to myself that I was in trouble, that I couldn't save myself. I had heard and prayed some amazing prayers over the years, but here I was like a child again. Just two words: "Help me." When I had no words left in me, these two words changed my life.

The Most Honest Prayer You Can Pray

One of the most honest, desperate prayers recorded in Scripture was that of a drowning man. Do you remember the story?

Immediately after this, Jesus insisted that his disciples get back into the boat and cross to the other side of the lake, while he sent the people home. After sending them home, he went up into the hills by himself to pray. Night fell while he was there alone.

Meanwhile, the disciples were in trouble far away from land, for a strong wind had risen, and they were fighting heavy waves. About three o'clock in the morning Jesus came toward them, walking on the water. When the disciples saw him walking on the water, they were terrified. In their fear, they cried out, "It's a ghost!"

But Jesus spoke to them at once. "Don't be afraid," he said. "Take courage. I am here!"

Then Peter called to him, "Lord, if it's really you, tell me to come to you, walking on the water."

"Yes, come," Jesus said.

So Peter went over the side of the boat and walked on the water toward Jesus. But when he saw the strong wind and the waves, he was terrified and began to sink. "Save me, Lord!" he shouted.

Jesus immediately reached out and grabbed him. "You have so little faith," Jesus said. "Why did you doubt me?" (Matt. 14:22–31)

The disciples were exhausted after a long, miraculous day on the hillside. Five thousand men (so probably a crowd of at least eight or nine thousand people counting women and children) had been fed with one boy's lunch. Not only that, but twelve baskets of food had been left over, one for each disciple. This was a visual message saying, "It's never been about you having enough; it will always be about Me being your more than enough." After the crowd had been fed, Jesus sent them away. He climbed up to the barren top of the mountain to be alone and pray after He had insisted that the disciples get in a boat and make the five-mile journey from Bethsaida to Gennesaret.

Soon the disciples were rowing into the wind, surrounded by high waves. Violent storms like this could descend on the Sea of Galilee without warning. It was 3:00 in the morning when they saw a figure walking toward them on the water. There were superstitious beliefs in those days that demons inhabited the water, and so the disciples were terrified to see someone walking on the surface of the waves. They thought the figure was a ghost, but Jesus immediately reassured them. "Don't be afraid. Take courage. I am here."

For the disciples, each day unveiled something new about Christ. They saw that He could turn water into the best wine. He could heal the sick. He could feed an army from almost nothing. But now this. He could walk on water. So Peter asked, "If it's really you, tell me to come to you." In response to those who wanted to see Jesus perform miracles as if He were a sideshow entertainer, Jesus refused, but to the small amount of faith that was growing in Peter, Jesus responded by saying, "Come." Peter put one leg over the side of the boat and then the other. Can you imagine what his friends thought as they watched him walk on water? We don't know how far he got or how far Jesus was from the boat, but when Peter took his eyes off Jesus for a moment and began to look around at the size of the waves, he panicked and began to sink. That night he prayed one of the most honest, desperate, powerful prayers any one of us can ever pray: "Save me, Lord!" Immediately, Jesus reached out and grabbed hold of him. Matthew goes on to tell us that "when they climbed back into the boat, the wind stopped" (v. 32).

Help me, Lord! Save me, Lord!

This kind of prayer acknowledges something that's always true but we're not always aware of: we cannot save ourselves. This is a prayer of absolute surrender. When I prayed that prayer through heaving sobs on the floor of my hospital room, the words of the psalm my beloved friend and mentor, Gilbert Kirby, had shared with me washed over me in waves:

> The Lord is close to the brokenhearted;
>   he rescues those whose spirits are crushed. (Ps. 34:18)

If that is you right now, I invite you to call out to Him. You don't need fancy words or even a lot of faith. Simply start right where you are. If you feel unclean, I remind you of Bobbie's words: Jesus's blood washes whiter than Tide or Persil. It really does.

I realize that some of you have walked with Jesus for a long time. Some of you are prayer warriors and intercessors, and I am so grateful for you. Thank you for your faithfulness. But some of you may have picked up this book because you tried praying in the past and it felt as if your prayers went no higher than the ceiling, so you simply stopped. Or you prayed for something that really mattered, something life changing, and God didn't answer, certainly not in any way that made sense to you. I ask, would you be willing to open your heart to the possibility of beginning again? I believe with everything in me that God wants to have a real relationship with you. Loving God is not about religion but relationship. Prayer is not about the right words; it's about the right heart. God knows you and loves you as you are, right now. You can start with a simple, "Help me, Lord!"

> *Loving God is not about religion but relationship. Prayer is not about the right words; it's about the right heart.*

> But in my distress I cried out to the LORD;
>   yes, I prayed to my God for help.
> He heard me from his sanctuary;
>   my cry to him reached his ears. (Ps. 18:6)

Even if you don't know what to say, just talk to God—He is listening.

Praying women know it's okay to start where they are.

PRAYER REMINDERS

1. Prayer is simply talking honestly with God.
2. When you don't know where to start, the simplest yet most powerful prayer is one word: Jesus.
3. Prayer is not about the right words; it's about the right heart.

A PRAYER WHEN YOU DON'T KNOW WHAT TO SAY

Father,

I don't have fancy words, but I have a heart that wants to know You better. Thank You that You are listening to every word. Amen.

TWO

Pray Because God
Is Waiting for You

Praying women believe that
God is listening right now.

Prayer is the most concrete way to make our home in God.

Henri Nouwen

Therefore the LORD waits to be gracious to you,
    and therefore he exalts himself to show mercy to you.
For the LORD is a God of justice;
    blessed are all those who wait for him.

Isaiah 30:18 ESV

I woke to the noise of our two dogs, Maggie and Tink, barking as if we had been invaded by a herd of cats. They were jumping up and down by the bedroom door, clearly frantic. I looked at my phone. It was just before 7:00

a.m. I reached over to wake Barry and realized that his side of the bed was empty. I was surprised. Whichever one of us wakes first in the morning always takes the dogs outside, so the fact that Barry wasn't there, and the dogs were, was unusual. I slipped out of bed, and as I reached the bedroom door, I stopped. I realized now why the dogs were barking. Loud noises were coming from downstairs. It sounded as if someone was turning our furniture over.

What's Barry doing? I wondered. Then a horrible thought crept into my mind. *What if it's not Barry? What if we're being robbed and they've knocked him out?*

I called his cell phone, and it went to voice mail. Not good. I looked around the bedroom for a potential weapon. All I could find was a pair of high-heeled boots.

I am dismally prepared for defense! I thought. *We should golf. I'm Scottish. I should have golf clubs up here.*

I decided I was overreacting. Perhaps Barry had taken the dogs out earlier and brought them back upstairs, and now he'd fallen over something, which is not unusual in our home. We are a family of trippers. I took one boot with me just in case. The moment I opened the bedroom door the dogs flew downstairs, barking all the way. Swinging my boot, I followed. We live in a three-level townhome, and when the dogs reached the ground floor, they stopped barking. That was either a really good sign or a really bad sign.

I called Barry's name.

Nothing.

I called again and heard a muffled, "Morning!"

I put my "weapon" down and made my way to the bottom level, where I found Barry and the dogs in the closet under the stairs up to their chins in boxes, blankets, and Christmas ornaments. This is our if-we-don't-know-where-to-put-it-we-throw-it-in-here closet.

"What are you doing?" I asked as I attempted to wade through the mess scattered all over the floor.

"I'm clearing out the closet," he said.

"At seven in the morning?" I asked. "Why? Where are we going to put all this stuff?"

"I don't know about that," he said. "But this . . ." There was a reverent pause as he gestured toward the closet. "This is our new prayer closet. I've been thinking about this for weeks, and here it is!"

"Wow!" I said. What else was there to say?

We spent the rest of that day finding new places to put the things we had no place for. Most of them ended up piled high in the garage or under the beds. I vacuumed up the glitter, and by that evening, Barry had the closet just the way he wanted it. He brought down his favorite devotional books, his Bible, and a journal. I liked the idea of a quiet place and joined "team prayer closet." I thought it would be good to have a specific place where we could close the door and each take time to be alone with God. Or so I thought.

On the first day, Barry realized that when you close the door, the light turns off, so he took in a flashlight with him. I didn't like that idea, so I brought in three candles, which worked until I knocked one over and set fire to my *Streams in the Desert* devotional.

The next day Barry prayed for a long time, so long that I was a little concerned. So I opened the door and found him fast asleep on the floor with the dogs curled up beside him.

By the end of week one, I had banged my head on the sloped ceiling twice, had needed to open the closet door to let the dogs in every time, and had discovered that I'm claustrophobic. Barry, sad to say, didn't fare any better. His prayer closet experiment had failed. Trying to find a holy place didn't work for us. But the truth is, God isn't looking for a holy place to meet with us. Because of Jesus, we are the holy place, and God is always waiting to meet with us, wherever we are.

In a closet.

In a shower.

In an office.

In a car.

As we walk the dog.

As we wait in line at the grocery store.

At a chemotherapy appointment.

Anywhere. Everywhere.

This truth is overwhelming. God invites you and me to come into His presence. Those who lived before the time of Christ could never have imagined such an invitation. In the Old Testament, people had no direct access to God. God is holy, and we are not. Yet God wanted His presence to be with His people, so He told Moses, "Have the people of Israel build me a holy sanctuary so I can live among them" (Exod. 25:8).

I don't know if you've ever seen a picture or a model of the temple; there was an outer court where the priests could go to offer sacrifices, but the Holy of Holies, where God's presence and His glory rested, could be accessed only once a year and only by the high priest. An embroidered veil, the width of a man's hand, separated the Holy Place from the Holy of Holies, but the life and death of Jesus changed everything. His last cry from the cross tore that embroidered veil in two.

> Then Jesus uttered another loud cry and breathed his last. And the curtain in the sanctuary of the Temple was torn in two, from top to bottom. (Mark 15:37–38)

I love that we read it was torn from top to bottom. Only God could have done that. He was saying to you and to me, "Come on in. I'm waiting for you." The barrier between God and humanity was torn in two.

> For we are the temple of the living God. As God said:
>   "I will live in them
>   and walk among them.
>   I will be their God,
>   and they will be my people." (2 Cor. 6:16)

Now I take my Bible and a cup of coffee outside, and I sit with my Father on my garden chair. Barry takes the dogs for a walk, and as he walks, he prays out loud when he thinks he's alone. It's quite a surprise to some of our neighbors. They think he's a little crazy. So far I've not been called as a witness!

The truth is there is no one right place to meet with God. You may have a prayer closet, and it's the perfect place for you. You may have a favorite chair to sit in or a place you love to walk. The bottom line is that wherever you choose, you'll discover that God is waiting for you. God is not waiting for a perfect place; you are the perfect place for God to live. God is not out there waiting for you to find Him; He is right here, with you right now when you call on His name.

> The LORD is close to all who call on him,
>   yes, to all who call on him in truth. (Ps. 145:18)

If you're still wondering where to begin, what to say, one of the most powerful, intimate prayers that I love that invites the presence of God is this: "Have mercy, God, on me."

The Prayer God Welcomes

Jesus talked a great deal about prayer. First, let's look at Luke 18, which tells a story about two men who saw themselves very differently in the eyes of God. One man thought he deserved God's love, and one didn't.

Jesus told this story. That might seem to be an obvious statement, but this fact is huge to me. The story doesn't convey just the thoughts of those who loved Jesus through the centuries. These are His words, His gift to us so we can learn about the kind of prayer God welcomes.

Let's look at the two men standing in very different places in the temple. Where they stand speaks volumes about who they are. One walked right in as if he were the guest of honor. The other held back; he wouldn't even lift his head. It's tempting to read the parable as a story for that time alone and miss what Jesus is saying. But when Jesus told a parable like this one, He was holding up a picture for everyone to see. Here He is illustrating two types of attitudes before God, two types of prayer:

1. going to God in self-righteousness
2. going to God broken and humble

37

Then Jesus told this story to some who had great confidence in their own righteousness and scorned everyone else: "Two men went to the Temple to pray. One was a Pharisee, and the other was a despised tax collector. The Pharisee stood by himself and prayed this prayer: 'I thank you, God, that I am not like other people—cheaters, sinners, adulterers. I'm certainly not like that tax collector! I fast twice a week, and I give you a tenth of my income.'

"But the tax collector stood at a distance and dared not even lift his eyes to heaven as he prayed. Instead, he beat his chest in sorrow, saying, 'O God, be merciful to me, for I am a sinner.' I tell you, this sinner, not the Pharisee, returned home justified before God. For those who exalt themselves will be humbled, and those who humble themselves will be exalted." (Luke 18:9–14)

The very devout in those days prayed three times a day, at 9:00 a.m., noon, and 3:00 p.m. It was believed that the most effective prayers were those offered in the temple, and that is where we meet these two men. The first thing that's clear from this story is that self-righteous people think God approves of them because of what they do and what they don't do. It's a me-centered religion. The Pharisee had no concept of his own need for the mercy of God because he was keeping the rules—not just keeping them but exceeding them. He made it clear in his prayer that he fasted twice a week even though Jews were required to fast only one day a year, on the Day of Atonement.

This is standard practice for you, a perpetual ordinance. On the tenth day of the seventh month, both the citizen and the foreigner living with you are to enter into a solemn fast and refrain from all work, because on this day atonement will be made for you, to cleanse you. In the presence of God you will be made clean of all your sins. It is a Sabbath of all Sabbaths. You must fast. It is a perpetual ordinance. (Lev. 16:29–31 Message)

The Pharisee was an overachiever! Those who wanted special merit with God through their own behavior fasted on Thursdays and Mondays. It was believed that Moses went up Mount Sinai to receive the Ten Commandments on a Thursday and came back down on a Monday, so these days were seen as holier than the others. Those who fasted on these days would whiten their faces and wander through Jerusalem in shabby clothes. As Mondays and Thursdays were market days, these people were assured of the largest audience to impress with their self-denial. The pride that many in the religious community saw as virtue in those days reeks of arrogance to us. One rabbi, Rabbi Simeon ben Jocai, is on record as saying, "If there are only two righteous men in the world, I and my son are these two; if there is only one, I am he!"[1]

For the Pharisee, thanking God that he wasn't an adulterer would have been wonderful if he had credited God for saving him from sinning, but that wasn't his heart. Notice how many times he uses the personal pronoun "I."

I thank you, God . . .

I am not like . . .

I'm certainly not like . . .

I fast . . .

I give . . .

His prayer is basically a love letter to himself. He has kept and exceeded all the rules because of his own strength, not because of the grace and mercy of God. As a Pharisee, he would have known the Psalms and the book of the prophet Isaiah, but he had missed their cries for mercy, the need for help and hope. I imagine he thought that King David should have called out for mercy because he was a sinner, an adulterer. He clearly missed that God called David a man after His own heart.

Having listed what he didn't do wrong, he commends himself for what he did right. He tithed all his income from everything, literally everything! Matthew recalls this indictment from Jesus: "What sorrow awaits you teachers of religious law and you Pharisees. Hypocrites! For you are careful to tithe even the tiniest income from your herb gardens, but you ignore the more important aspects of the law—justice, mercy, and faith" (Matt. 23:23).

If you purchased your basil and thyme from this man for five dollars, fifty cents went to the Lord. This was good and right if the act came from a grateful heart, but because the Pharisee believed his actions made him right with God, he had missed the message of the gospel. The Pharisee would be offended to think that God was not impressed with his prayer. It would make no sense to him.

Although I don't like the Pharisee represented here, I see a bit of myself in him. For too many years, I tried to keep all the rules to please God. This came from a broken place, a place of wanting to be loved so badly that I did everything in my power to impress God. I wanted to be perfect. I didn't see this as pride. I thought being perfect would make God love me more. No matter where our pride comes from, though, it separates us from God.

Whether we think we are so good that we've gained God's approval or too bad for God's love depends on how we view God. This is such a huge issue that I want to stay here for a moment. Think about your own life. When you pray, how do you go to God? What are your thoughts about whether He hears you or not? A. W. Tozer, in his masterful work *The Pursuit of God*, wrote this: "What comes into our minds when we think about God is the most important thing about us."[2]

When you think about God, what comes to your mind? Do you think God is pleased or displeased with you? If He is pleased, why? And if not, why not?

I have a friend who is struggling with an addiction at the moment. She'll do really well for a while and then fall again. We've had conversations about what's happening in her heart in the middle of this battle. When she's doing well, she feels that God is cheering her on, and when she falls, she feels as if He's shaking His head in disappointment and she stops praying. It is so hard for us to grasp that God's love for us is never based on our performance. It is based on the finished work of Christ, and that never changes. Now, is God pleased when she's doing well? I'm sure He is, but His pleasure springs from His love for her; it is not based on a score He keeps for or against her.

God wants us all to make choices that lead to life, but when we fall, His love remains the same. This makes no earthly sense to us because we'll never experience that kind of love anywhere but at the throne of grace and mercy. If we are able with the help of the Holy Spirit to begin to grasp hold of this truth, it will change not only how we see ourselves but also how we see others. The Pharisee distanced himself from the tax collector not realizing that he was actually distancing himself from God. Until you've had your heart broken, you can't see yourself or others the way God does. I know this from the place of my own breaking.

When I worked in television, hosting a Christian talk show, I did everything I could to be someone God would be proud of. I went in early and stayed late. If someone needed my help, I was there. I pushed myself to the breaking point in my need for God's approval. You can kill yourself with drugs and alcohol and know deep down inside that you're ruining your life, but you can also kill yourself working for God and think it's holy. When my life fell apart and I ended up in a psychiatric ward, I knew I had failed. I found myself, bloodied and bruised in my soul, on the floor, waiting for God to wipe me out because I'd let Him down. Instead, He sat with me, comforted me, and welcomed me home to His heart because He had loved me all along. I knew then that He would have held me closer sooner, but everything I had done to make Him love me had gotten in the way. I experienced not only the love of God in a more profound way but also the love of others.

> *You can kill yourself with drugs and alcohol and know deep down inside that you're ruining your life, but you can also kill yourself working for God and think it's holy.*

I don't know how this idea sits with you at this moment in your life. If you get it, I'm so happy for you. If it seems too good to be true or even just sounds wrong, I long for you to know that you can go as you are to God, who is waiting to welcome you.

The second man, the one Jesus said went home justified before God, was the one who was painfully aware of his sin. Unlike the Pharisee, the tax collector stood at the back in the temple courtyard. He didn't march to the front as if he had a right to be there; he stood with his eyes cast down. It's interesting that Jesus said he "beat his chest in sorrow." Such an act was viewed in Middle Eastern eyes as true contrition or repentance. This is significant because the source of the spiritual life is the heart.

> I have stored up your word in my heart,
>   that I might not sin against you. (Ps. 119:11 ESV)

> Guard your heart above all else,
>   for it determines the course of your life. (Prov. 4:23)

> Search me, O God, and know my heart;
>   test me and know my anxious thoughts. (Ps. 139:23)

The Pharisee saw others as sinners; the tax collector saw only one sinner standing before God: himself. He prayed a prayer of humility and desperation. He kept his eyes low, but his prayers ascended to the throne of grace. "O God, be merciful to me, for I am a sinner." His prayer did not contain even a moment of justification, no "I know I blew it on Tuesday, but Wednesday was stellar!" All he offered in the presence of a holy God was a broken and contrite heart.

The people who were listening to Jesus's story would have been right with Him up to this point. Everything was in order as far as they could tell. The "good" man offered up his good prayer, and the "bad" man offered up the only prayer a bad man could offer, but once more, Jesus was about to turn the tables on them.

> I tell you, this sinner, not the Pharisee, returned home justified before God. For those who exalt themselves will be humbled, and those who humble themselves will be exalted. (Luke 18:14)

This went against everything they understood about God. Jewish people were raised under "the burden of the law." There were 613 laws laid out in the Old Testament. They were divided into "positive" and "negative" laws, things to do and things to avoid. There were 365 don'ts and 248 do's (which interestingly enough is the number of days in the year and the number of bones in the human body, respectively. In this way, the Jewish people were called to obey the law every day with their entire bodies.)[3] The crowd was shocked when Jesus said that the one returning home justified was the sinner. Everything they knew about what was pleasing to God had been turned upside down. It was Luke 15 all over again.

When Jesus told the story of the prodigal son, those listening saw only one villain, the son who disrespected his father, asked for his share of the family inheritance, and left home. When he dared to return to a community that traditionally would have met him at the gate, forbidding him ever to return, Jesus changed the ending. The father in the story ran. Unheard of. Undignified. He reached the boy before the crowd could touch him and he welcomed him home—full honors, no shame. The crowd listening that day would have been stunned. The religious leaders would have been deeply offended, while the disenfranchised and broken would have seen a glimmer of hope for their lives.

If you're looking for a faith that makes sense, Christianity will leave you offended, confused, and stripped of every good thing you have to say about yourself. But if you're looking for a faith in which you are invited to come as you are, be showered with mercy and compassion, a faith in which you will be loved back to life again, welcome home. The Father is waiting. Always waiting.

Before my life fell apart and I ended up in a psychiatric ward, I was very conscious of my own performance as a believer. Even as I type that, I wish it weren't true, but it was. I had no deep assurance that God loved me just for me, and I was very careful about everything I did. After the fall, I was free . . . almost.

Come and Sit for a While

There are still some situations that expose my brokenness. I can stand on a platform and speak to twenty thousand people and not be nervous at all.

I know why they're there. They're there because they want God to touch them. They're there because they want to hear from God and be encouraged. They long for hope and help. I get it now that I am simply the earthly vessel the hope flows through. It's Jesus who changes lives, and I can't wait to tell others about Him. But put me in front of a photographer, and I'm not so comfortable. Part of that discomfort is that before any photo shoot, I always determine that I'm going to lose ten pounds, and I usually end up gaining five . . . or more. It's ridiculous, I know, but there you go. I still see myself in many ways as the teenage girl with bad skin and greasy hair, and instead of helping her out, I sabotage her efforts with two of my friends, Ben and Jerry. I wonder if you've ever done that? It's almost like we're afraid to let ourselves win. Instead, over and over, we set ourselves up to fail. Then we get mad at ourselves and pick up that overcoat of shame that's never far out of reach. The truth remains that God is not mad at us and the overcoat doesn't belong to us. Jesus wore it on the cross.

In the spring of 2019, Barry and I drove to a little town in Texas for a photo shoot for this book. I'd never met the photographer, but I'd seen pictures of the place where we'd be shooting. It was a large white barn that's usually used for weddings. That morning our local weather guy predicted the worst storms we'd had in Texas all year. He said we'd see hailstones the size of baseballs. I suggested to Barry that we reschedule the shoot. He suggested that I get in the car.

The drive took a little less time than we thought it would, so we arrived before the photographer and the rest of the team. While Barry was unloading some things from the car, I went inside. It took my breath away. It looked more like a church than a barn. All the wood was painted white. It had high ceilings and was flooded with natural light from the windows. Barry had brought a white chair from home, and he set it in the middle of the room, then went back to the car to grab my garment bag. There was silence in the room, and for a moment, the sun burst through the rain clouds, casting a golden glow on the white chair sitting in the middle of this vast, empty space, and in my spirit, I heard my Father say, "Come and sit for a while." He had been waiting all along. I sat there, loved.

It's hard to fully explain, but the emptier my hands have become before God, the fuller my heart has become. The invitation is for every one of us.

Be still, and know that I am God! (Ps. 46:10)

Step out of the traffic! Take a long, loving look at me, your High God, above politics, above everything. (Ps. 46:10 Message)

Let's pause here for a moment and let the love of God surround us. I know that your life is crazy busy and that the idea of being still is number thirty-six on your to-do list, but you were made for more.

As I sat on the chair that day in the stillness, everything else took a backseat. Yes, my jeans were still a little tight, but who cares. My sweater was long enough to cover my lack of willpower. Instead, I was reminded of how God sees me—loved, chosen, bought with the greatest price anyone has ever paid for anything. The same is true of you. Don't sit in the dark; let the light of God's love in.

You Are Welcome Here

I didn't see her until they put up the lights for the morning break. The church was full, apart from the back row on the left, where one woman sat alone. When the lights came up, she grabbed her purse and made her way into the lobby. I wondered why she was by herself. Later that day, I saw her again. She was sitting on a bench outside the church. I'd slipped out a side door to get a little fresh air, and when I saw her, I walked over to where she sat and asked if I could join her. She moved her purse, and I sat down. We didn't say anything for a few moments, but then she told me that she'd driven four hours to come to the conference. I thanked her for coming and asked if there was no one who could have come with her and shared the drive. She smiled a sad little smile and said that she knew all the women in the front two rows. They were all from the church where she used to be a member. I asked her why she wasn't sitting with them.

She took a deep breath and looked down at her feet. Her story is one I've heard over and over, slightly different circumstances but in essence the same: a fall from grace.

"I'm not welcome where I am known," she said. There's a lot more to her story, but it's hers to tell, not mine. As we sat on the bench that day, she allowed me to pray for her as she cried out to God for mercy. I had the joy of reminding her that the one place where she is known and always welcome is in the presence of her Father. He is waiting, always waiting. What troubled her the most was that she knew what she was doing was wrong when she did it, and she did it anyway. I reminded her that that's why Jesus came. Jesus didn't give His life for those who feel they have the right to march right up to the front of the temple and list off everything they've done right. Jesus came for those who sit in the back row crying out, "Be merciful to me, a sinner."

Sometimes it's our sin that keeps us from praying. Sometimes it's our busyness. Sometimes it's because we're not sure that God is listening. God is waiting for you. He is listening. Whether you are in a quiet prayer closet, on a walk in the woods, or sitting in a chair right in the middle of the largest space in your home, let God's love flow over you. He is waiting. Come as you are.

Praying women believe that God is listening right now.

PRAYER REMINDERS

1. Right now, God invites you to come as you are.
2. God is waiting and listening.
3. Pray with humility, asking God for His mercy.

A PRAYER TO REMIND YOU THAT GOD IS WAITING FOR YOU

Father,

Thank You that You are waiting for me. My mind is busy. My thoughts take me in so many directions. Teach me to be still with You. Help me to know Your love. Help me to come to You like a child with empty hands before You. Fill my heart right now with Your presence. I will wait with You. In Jesus's name I pray, amen.

THREE

Pray . . . and Don't Give Up

*Praying women never stop praying
until they receive God's answer.*

Our motto must continue to be perseverance. And ultimately I trust
the Almighty will crown our efforts with success.

William Wilberforce

So I say to you, ask and keep on asking, and it will be given to you; seek
and keep on seeking, and you will find; knock and keep on knocking,
and the door will be opened to you. For everyone who keeps on asking
[persistently], receives; and he who keeps on seeking [persistently],
finds; and to him who keeps on knocking [persistently], the door will
be opened.

Luke 11:9–10 AMP

I've always been a tomboy. I was not one of those girls who knew from the
time they held their first doll that they were made to be a mother. I loved
other people's children, but I never felt as if I had to have children of my

own. I wanted a dog. When I became an aunt for the first time, I was excited to hold that darling baby boy, but I was equally excited to hand him back to my sister when he started to wail with enough intensity to terrify the cat. Instinctively, she knew just what to do. Some women seem to come with the natural-born-mother gene. I have a friend who has thirteen children. Thirteen! No twins, no one is adopted, just pregnant thirteen times. I asked once how she keeps track of them all, as they live way out in the country. She told me that she counts their shoes at the door. What a woman!

I didn't meet my husband, Barry, until I was thirty-seven. He is seven years younger than me, which he reminds me of on a fairly regular basis. I had watched him with his nieces and nephews and knew that he loved children and that his chances of having a large family with me were not good unless we fostered or adopted. I remember telling him that he might want to find someone younger than me. He rejected that idea and we were married on a beautiful snowy day in December in Charleston, South Carolina. Once we were married, we took the business of getting pregnant very seriously, but as happens to many women, each passing month was another disappointment. After a year of trying, I went to my doctor to see if conceiving was even possible for me. She was very positive and encouraging. Her nurse was less so. "All your eggs will be hard-boiled by now!"

For the first time in my life, I found myself longing for a child. Every time I passed a mom in the mall or in the grocery store with her little ones felt like a stab to my heart. These women belonged to a community that I might never be invited into. I begged God to give us a child. When I prayed, I told Him that if He would give me just one child, I would love him or her with every fiber of my being. And then it happened! When I saw the positive sign on the pregnancy test, I dropped it. It lay wrong way up on the bathroom floor, and I was afraid to pick it up in case it was wrong. I drove to the drugstore and bought another one. Again it said I was pregnant. I still wasn't sure as I'd eaten a lot of carbs the night before, so I drove back and bought one more. The girl at the cash register said, "Accept it, honey, you're pregnant." She was right.

I didn't know how to tell Barry. I thought I should probably have a parade and a brass band and balloons, but as he was due home from work in forty minutes, I had to scrap those ideas. Instead, I set the table for dinner with candles and fresh flowers, and I put the pregnancy test onto his dinner plate covered by a silver dome. I had the reveal all planned out. We would start with a salad, and I'd ask about his day. I would then bring out the pièce de résistance and set it in front of him. But instead, the moment he walked in, my perfect plan went down the drain and I yelled, "We're pregnant!"

When What You've Asked For Goes Wrong

The first few weeks of my pregnancy were a blur of absolute joy. I told complete strangers that I was pregnant. I read books to the wee one in my belly and played an assortment of songs to see if he or she was more country or pop. At our sonogram, we learned the baby was a boy. We were so happy.

Then one phone call interrupted our happiness. I would be forty years old when the baby was born, and my doctor had asked for additional tests, one being an amniocentesis. When the results came back, she asked us to come to her office. We sat on one side of her desk as she sat on the other with a brown folder in front of her. I don't remember everything she said, but I remember this: "Your baby is incompatible with life."

I stared at her as if she was speaking in a foreign language. This was a phrase I'd never heard before. Neither Barry nor I said anything. We were stunned. She went on to explain about "markers" and "abnormalities" and what my results showed. I could see her mouth moving, but I felt as if I had a glass dome over my head and couldn't hear her. Then she said that she recommended performing a termination the following day. I heard that, and her words snapped me back into reality. I was shocked. "No!" I said vehemently. "No! Absolutely not. This little one will have every day God has planned for him to live."

We drove home in silence. There was nothing to say. For the next couple of weeks, I was tormented with one thought: I had begged God to give me a child, and now He was going to take him away before we had a chance to love him. Why? I felt as if I were falling into a dark hole. Some days I felt angry, others I was overwhelmed with sorrow. One day turned the tide for me.

I woke up early and drove to the beach, as we were living in Southern California at the time. The beach was deserted; my only companions were seagulls. I took off my shoes and walked to the edge of the water and prayed. I prayed like I had never prayed before, out loud to the wind and the waves and the birds.

Jesus! My heart is aching. I don't understand this at all, but I just want to declare here and now that we are in this together. I've always needed You, but I know right now that I need You more than I ever have. I don't know how this will end, but I'm not letting go of You for one moment. You didn't promise me happiness, but You did promise You would never leave me. I'm not letting go. I'm not giving up. You and me—we're in this together.

Something shifted inside me. I had no idea how long I could carry our son, but I became relentless in my prayers, not for a perfect outcome but for the presence of a perfect Father. At thirty-five weeks, my doctor called. I held my breath. She told me that the day my results had come back the results of another forty-year-old patient had also come back. My results had gone into her chart and hers into mine. There had never been anything wrong with our son. I fell to my knees and thanked God, but then I prayed for the other mother who would be getting a very different phone call. I believe in the sovereignty of God, and I've often wondered if I was allowed to carry her burden for a while. I don't know the answer to that, but I do know that when my heart was breaking, I learned to hold on to God as I never had before in my life.

I don't know what battle you are facing right now. It may be for your child, your marriage, your health, or your very sanity, but what I want you to know is this: when we pray and refuse to give up, no matter how long an answer takes, things change. If you are discouraged, let me say, in Jesus's name, hold on! The enemy would love nothing more than for us to give up and stop praying. Jesus graciously gifted us with the following parable to make it clear that no matter how hard the place is that you find yourself in right now, no matter how long the night of suffering and struggle we are going through, we should never, never stop praying.

The Woman Who Wouldn't Walk Away

One of the most powerful illustrations Jesus gave of what it looks like to pray and pray and never give up is the story of a widow who wouldn't go away.

> One day Jesus told his disciples a story to show that they should always pray and never give up. "There was a judge in a certain city," he said, "who neither feared God nor cared about people. A widow of that city came to him repeatedly, saying, 'Give me justice in this dispute with my enemy.' The judge ignored her for a while, but finally he said to himself, 'I don't fear God or care about people, but this woman is driving me crazy. I'm going to see that she gets justice, because she is wearing me out with her constant requests!'"
>
> Then the Lord said, "Learn a lesson from this unjust judge. Even he rendered a just decision in the end. So don't you think God will surely give justice to his chosen people who cry out to him day and night? Will he keep putting them off? I tell you, he will grant justice to them quickly! But when the Son of Man returns, how many will he find on the earth who have faith?" (Luke 18:1–8)

This one parable unpacks so much about prayer. Imagine right now that you are sitting at Jesus's feet wrestling with your battles and He takes your lovely face in His hands and lets you in on a kingdom secret, telling you how to pray when you are overwhelmed and ready to quit. You may have been fighting your battles for so long and are tempted to believe that God is not listening, that He doesn't care. I pray that this passage puts those thoughts to rest. God is listening to you. He cares about you. Look at what Jesus said. I love the way Luke spells it out for us:

> One day Jesus told his disciples a story to show that they should always pray and never give up. (18:1)

Not a lot of mystery there. It's crystal clear. Sometimes Jesus's parables were difficult for those who were listening to understand. Not here. Jesus wants us to know that persistent prayer matters. Persistent prayer changes things. This kind of prayer is not a "God, bless my son" prayer. This is a down-on-your-knees, fully-engaged-in-battle, refusing-to-give-up-until-God-answers kind of prayer.

Jesus makes a comparison between a judge who should be willing to help a poor widow but won't give her the time of day and God, a loving Father who is moved by the cries of His people. In this parable, the judge doesn't care about God or about standing before Him one day. He is the definition of a law unto himself. Hearing that this judge not only doesn't fear God but also has no regard for people allows us to make a few assumptions about him. A man like this is open to the worst kind of corruption and bribery. If you want justice from him, you'll need to make it worth his while. So a widow, with little to no status or money in that society, had no hope.

In contrast, God tells us all to come as we are with empty, open hands and that He will hear our cry and answer. Our culture is obsessed with money and status and social media followers. We might be tempted to feel as if we have no significant voice in this world. If we're not careful, though, we can let this feeling spill over into our relationship with God. Perhaps you expect God to hear the prayers of your pastor or those you look up to in the faith, those with significant platforms, but you put yourself at the bottom of God's to-do list. That is not the case. You are not at the bottom of God's to-do list; you are right at the top. God doesn't care whether you've written a book or spoken at a conference or anything else you might attach significance to. He waits to hear from you. He cares about you. He loves you.

I saw that kind of confident assurance in the faith of my mother. As a single mum raising three children, she had very limited resources. She often depended on the kindness of friends from our church for food for special occasions such as Christmas or for clothes for a growing tribe (like my brother's pants), but when we gathered together to pray, she didn't go to God as a poor widow begging for help. She went as a daughter of the King to her Father. She didn't go to a judge who saw her as one more insignificant beggar; she went to the King of heaven, whose door was always open to her. One thing I knew about my mum was that she was persistent, relentless in prayer, and this was based on her relationship with her Father.

Many of you have written to me about where you find yourself right now. Some of you have lost income, or a husband has walked away. One letter that broke my heart was from a woman who had gained weight and was still single and believed no one would ever want to be with her. Whatever your story is, please remember that even if every other door is slammed in your face, the door into your Father's presence never, ever will be. Don't skip over that. We get used to seeing encouraging phrases as memes or bumper stickers, but this is a life-changing truth. The One who holds the universe in place, who sits on the eternal throne, to whom one day every knee will bow and every tongue will confess that He is Lord loves you! You are not forgotten and not overlooked; you are seen and loved and listened to. That's why Jesus tells us not to lose heart.

In the parable, Jesus makes the point that even a corrupt judge will eventually give in to this woman who refuses to quit, simply because he wants to get rid of her. Every time he steps out his front door, there she is again! How much more will your Father who loves you respond to your fervent prayers?

Sometimes we believe the lack of a speedy answer to our prayers means God is ignoring them or not even hearing them. We live in a quick-fix world in which we expect immediate answers. If we're on hold with the telephone company for more than a few minutes, we want to hang up. (Don't ask me how I know this!) As God's daughters, we need to renew our minds about what is eternal truth and what is popularly held belief. Persistence, commitment, and intentional prayer are profoundly spiritual values. We are losing them in our Christian community; instead, we want instant worship and short messages so we can get home for an afternoon nap.

I watched with the rest of the world in horror as flames shot through the roof of Notre Dame Cathedral in Paris. Donations flooded in to rebuild this historic place of worship, but a comment from a French priest on the news that evening was very telling. He said that the kind of artisans who built cathedrals in the past no longer exist. Most of them never saw the work finished in their lifetimes. They gave their lives to something that was bigger than themselves, and no one seems to want to do that anymore.

God is calling His warrior women to invest their lives in something that is bigger than themselves: the kingdom of God. These kinds of women give their lives to relentless prayer.

What Will Jesus Find?

The last verse in the parable about the persistent widow is very significant:

> But when the Son of Man returns, how many will he find on the earth who have faith? (Luke 18:8)

As this is found at the end of a parable on prayer, the text indicates that when Christ returns, He will equate faith with those who persisted in prayer. He will find some of us who prayed and then quit because it got too hard and some who refused to quit no matter how hard it got. The question is this: How many will He find who persisted in prayer? This kind of prayer life is not based on results but on faith in Christ. I've been both kinds of people. I've prayed during situations that were difficult and heartbreaking, and other times I just gave up. The load felt like too much, and I quit. Perhaps I quit because I was carrying the load myself instead of bringing it to the throne of grace and mercy every single day. Now I'm learning—and this parable has helped me—to pray and pray and pray until I feel as if God must be fed up hearing from me but I know He's not.

Even If Your Friends Fail You

Luke recounts the second story Jesus told about being persistent in prayer.

> Then He said to them, "Suppose one of you has a friend, and goes to him at midnight and says, 'Friend, lend me three loaves [of bread]; for a friend of mine who is on a journey has just come to visit me, and I have nothing to serve him'; and from inside he answers, 'Do not bother me; the door has already been shut and my children and I are in bed; I cannot get up and give you anything.' I tell you, even though he will not get up and give him anything

just because he is his friend, yet because of his persistence and boldness he will get up and give him whatever he needs.

"So I say to you, ask and keep on asking, and it will be given to you; seek and keep on seeking, and you will find; knock and keep on knocking, and the door will be opened to you. For everyone who keeps on asking [persistently], receives; and he who keeps on seeking [persistently], finds; and to him who keeps on knocking [persistently], the door will be opened." (Luke 11:5–10 AMP)

Before we unpack this story, I want to draw your attention to how this chapter in Luke begins. It starts with a request from the disciples.

It happened that while Jesus was praying in a certain place, after He finished, one of His disciples said to Him, "Lord, teach us to pray just as John also taught his disciples." (Luke 11:1 AMP)

I've always thought of John the Baptist as a prophet crying out in the wilderness, but Jesus's disciples thought of John as a man of prayer. Just as Isaac was a miracle born to Abraham and Sarah in their old age, John was a miracle born to his parents, Zechariah and Elizabeth. Both are described as advanced in age, and Elizabeth was called barren. John was a miracle baby who was filled with the Holy Spirit before he was born, but he was also a man of prayer. He was the one given the privilege of baptizing Jesus. He knew he had just baptized the Messiah, but he didn't think, *Job done.* He continued to be a man of prayer. He saw and heard things we can only imagine.

Then John testified, "I saw the Holy Spirit descending like a dove from heaven and resting upon him. I didn't know he was the one, but when God sent me to baptize with water, he told me, 'The one on whom you see the Spirit descend and rest is the one who will baptize with the Holy Spirit.' I saw this happen to Jesus, so I testify that he is the Chosen One of God." (John 1:32–34 AMP)

If John, who saw so much, was a man of prayer, how much more should we be?

It's interesting too that Jesus's disciples didn't ask him how to heal the sick or raise the dead. They didn't ask how to put a good three-point sermon together. They asked Jesus to teach them how to pray. We'll look at the Lord's Prayer in another chapter, but for now, let's look at how he responded to their question.

Jesus told a story about someone showing up on a friend's doorstep at midnight looking for sandwiches. Jesus makes it clear that the person in the house was a friend, not a stranger or a callous judge but a friend.

> Even though he will not get up and give him anything just because he is his friend. (Luke 11:8 AMP)

Again, in this parable, the main point is about persistence in prayer, but another message is tucked into the folds. The friend eventually gets up, but not based on friendship. He gets up because he wants to go back to sleep! Jesus is acknowledging that at times, whether we mean to or not, we will let one another down.

I know you've been there. Perhaps you've gone through a painful divorce and you need your friends to understand the depth of the hurt, the loneliness, the burden of raising your children alone. For a time, they are right there, but then life goes on and they are caught up in their own lives and families. It's easy to feel forgotten, passed over. Or if you suffer with a medical condition, initially your friends can't do enough for you, but then time drags on and they're not there as often as they were. Perhaps you need them more now than you did in the beginning, but you feel as if they have moved on.

We will never be enough for one another. The human heart is so complicated, so deep, and wounds from the past can present themselves at the least expected time and drag us down. What Jesus is saying here is that this is reality. Our friends and families will never be all we need, and we will never be all they need. But Jesus is always more than enough. He is always more than we need. And He will always be there.

One of the things I fight is isolation. I used to think this was because of my battle with depression, but I think it's more than that. When people experience any kind of abuse in childhood, they respond in different ways. Because my experience was physical abuse from my dad before he took his own life, I became very self-protective. I didn't expect anyone to help me. I would have to help myself. I remember seeing the movie *Cinderella* as a young girl with a bunch of my friends for a birthday treat. They loved it, and I hated it. My reaction was so strong because the idea that a prince was coming to rescue me contradicted everything I had experienced in life thus far.

I have to be careful even now not to slip back into that self-protective place when I'm at my most vulnerable. I was very raw after my mum's death and felt that one of my closest friends who should have understood how much I was hurting simply wasn't there for me. As weeks passed without hearing from her, I went into that "who needs you" mode, which is not very attractive for a mature Christian. But slipping back into old ways of thinking is so easy. What I'm learning is that part of praying when we want to quit is bringing all of

> *Part of praying when we want to quit is bringing all of who we are to Christ and not giving up.*

who we are to Christ and not giving up. As a child, I believed that no one was coming to rescue me. I was wrong. There is a Prince, and His name is Jesus.

God Is for You

What would you ask Jesus for if you could see Him? If He was sitting right across from you at your kitchen table, listening, inviting you to ask for anything that was on your heart, what would you ask for? Why don't you make a list? Be as specific as you can. See Him there, arms open wide, eyes full of the kind of love that changes everything. We struggle to have an accurate picture of that love. We've never experienced it anywhere, and so to be invited to come and be welcomed with abandon feels wrong. It sounds too good to be true. We know too much about ourselves. But there is nothing we have ever done, no secret we can keep, no shame we've buried that He doesn't know about.

When I'm speaking at a conference, I often ask women to imagine that there's been a change of plan. Instead of listening to me speak, they are going to watch a movie of their lives—everything they've ever done, everything they've ever said, director's cut, nothing left out. Then I ask them as I ask you, How would that make you feel? Take a moment to reflect on that. For most of us, the thought is horrifying. But the truth of the gospel is that God has seen your movie and loves you anyway. How would really believing that change your life? Holding these two things together is radical. One, God knows every single thing about us, the good, the bad, and the very ugly. Two, He waits for us with open arms of love. Jesus told so many stories to help those listening to understand that God was not out to punish them or to trick them but to love them.

Right after Jesus's admonition to ask, seek, knock in Luke 11, He says this: "What father among you, if his son asks for a fish, will instead of a fish give him a serpent; or if he asks for an egg, will give him a scorpion?" (vv. 11–12 ESV). When Matthew recounts the story, he adds one more thing: "If your children ask for a loaf of bread, do you give them a stone instead?" (Matt. 7:9).

Those listening to Jesus that day pictured different visuals than you and I would. The things Jesus compared were very similar to each other, and the people knew that. Eels live in the Sea of Galilee, and they were most likely what Jesus was referring to as a serpent. Eels were forbidden by Jewish dietary law, so the question was, "What father if his son asks for a fish will trick him and give him something he can't eat? Or what father if his son asks for an egg will give him a scorpion?" There is a kind of scorpion that is pale in color, and when it's at rest, it tucks its tail and claws in and looks a little like an egg. What father will give that to his child? If your child is hungry and asks for an egg, will you give him something that will sting and harm him? The small limestone rocks on the edge of the Sea of Galilee are the same shape as small loaves of bread, but who will give them to their son as food?

Every year on Christian's birthday, I pray for that woman I never met, the one whose results went in my chart and mine in hers. I wasn't allowed to know who she was or what happened to her pregnancy, but I ask God to wrap His arms of love around her. And as for Christian . . . he turns twenty-four in December, and I'm still praying!

God is not out to trick us or to harm us. Persisting in prayer no matter how hard it is or how long an answer takes will happen only when we believe that God is who He says He is. If we doubt His love, we will hold back in prayer. If we believe in and receive that love, we will dive in with everything we have and are. Perhaps that's why I love the ocean so much. When I look out at the vast expanse, I get a tiny glimpse of God's vast love.

Persisting in prayer no matter how hard it is or how long an answer takes will happen only when we believe that God is who He says He is.

> Here is love, vast as the ocean,
> loving-kindness as the flood,
> when the Prince of Life, our Ransom,
> shed for us His precious blood.
> Who His love will not remember?
> Who can cease to sing His praise?
> He can never be forgotten
> throughout heaven's eternal days.
>
> William Rees[1]

Praying women
never stop
praying until
they receive
God's answer.

PRAYER REMINDERS

1. Pray with boldness and don't give up.
2. When you pray, believe that Jesus is enough for whatever you are facing.
3. Persist in prayer because you know that God is who He says He is.

A PRAYER WHEN YOU WANT TO GIVE UP

Father,

I want to be relentless in prayer. I don't want to give up. I want to ask and keep asking. I want to seek and keep seeking. I want to knock and keep knocking. Sometimes I lose heart. Sometimes I lose hope. But I want to be the kind of woman who prays through to an answer. Holy Spirit, keep me standing strong. For Jesus's sake, amen.

FOUR

Pray Hardest When It's Hardest to Pray

*Praying women press through
in prayer even when life is tough.*

When we pray for the Spirit's help . . . we will simply fall down at the
Lord's feet in our weakness. There we will find the victory and power
that comes from His love.

Andrew Murray

He went on a little farther and fell to the ground. He prayed that,
if it were possible, the awful hour awaiting him might pass him by.
"Abba, Father," he cried out, "everything is possible for you. Please
take this cup of suffering away from me. Yet I want your will to be
done, not mine."

Mark 14:35–36

I've been on a diet for forty years. I've lost and gained back the same ten or
fifteen pounds over and over and over again. I call them "homing pounds,"

as they always find their way back home. That might not seem like a lot of weight, but on my frame, it feels like a lot. Some people gain weight a little bit all over, so it's not as obvious. Not me. I get fat knees. No woman wants fat knees. No woman who lives in Texas where it's so hot you can cook a rib-eye steak on the sidewalk wants fat knees. You can find me really quickly in a crowd in the summer. I'm the only one not wearing shorts!

Name a diet, I've done it . . . several times. I've eaten cabbage soup until I almost lost the will to live. I've eaten steak and chicken and nothing else, and still those little keto strips refused to change color. The truth is that all the different diets work; it's me that doesn't. Halfway through day one after I've committed to a new diet, I'm already thinking, *I think I liked that other diet better*. So when Barry told me that he was going to follow the Daniel Fast for twenty-one days, my ears perked up. He explained, however, that this had nothing to do with a diet or my knees; it was a commitment he was making to get closer to God and to go deeper in prayer. I could tell Barry was serious. He was determined to pursue God no matter how uncomfortable it was or how much he longed for Chick-fil-A.

Get Serious

Have you ever experienced times in life when you needed to take prayer to the next level? You were being persistent, relentless, but the burden you were carrying wasn't getting any lighter. And then you realized that more than an answer to prayer, what you really wanted was the presence of God. That's what Barry communicated to me. He had felt for some time that he'd lost some of the joy in his relationship with God, and when he prayed, God felt distant. Praying was hard. He needed a breakthrough and believed that the Daniel Fast might provide one. I don't know if you are familiar with this fast. There appear to be various versions and levels of commitment, but Barry went all in.

> When this vision came to me, I, Daniel, had been in mourning for three whole weeks. All that time I had eaten no rich food. No meat or wine crossed

my lips, and I used no fragrant lotions until those three weeks had passed. (Dan. 10:2–3)

For twenty-one days, Barry ate vegetables and brown rice and no sugar or salt. He drank only water; no coffee and no soda. He is a huge devotee of a certain soda, so this was a big deal for him. He was serious in his desire to press into God's presence. The impact as the fast progressed, however, surprised him. For several mornings, he woke up with a name and a face in his mind. Sometimes they were accompanied by an overwhelming call to pray for that person, and he would drop to his knees and pray. At other times, the Holy Spirit told him to forgive someone who had wounded him in the past. Even though he thought he had forgiven them, it was as if the Holy Spirit was doing a spiritual deep clean. Barry prayed hardest when it was hardest to pray.

An answered prayer might give information, but God's presence gives peace no matter what the answer is.

"I wasn't asking for an answer from God," he told me. "I was asking for God Himself."

That rang true deep inside me. There are times in life when an answer isn't enough; we need the overwhelming presence of God. An answered prayer might give information, but God's presence gives peace no matter what the answer is. In my own life, I was about to discover how much I needed that peace.

Not This, Lord!

I travel a lot. I've flown more than three million miles on one airline alone. Suffice it to say, at times I get very tired, but on this particular day, it felt like more than simple travel fatigue. I had the worst headache ever. I had never had a migraine before, but this sure felt like one. It was as if there was an iron band around my head and it was slowly being tightened. I took two Advil and lay down on my bed with the lights off, but the pain didn't lift at all. I called my doctor's office to see if I could get an appointment that day, but they were swamped with a recent flu epidemic. So Barry decided to take me to a local drop-in medical clinic. We waited for a while before a young nurse took me back to a treatment room. My blood pressure was sky-high, which was a little concerning, but I thought that if I had the flu, that might affect it. When the doctor came in, he commented on my blood pressure, then asked me what my main complaint was. I told him I had a terrible headache, and he asked what I now know to be a key medical question: "Is this the worst headache you've ever had?"

I told him it was. The next question changed the atmosphere in the room. "Has anyone in your family ever had an aneurysm?"

When I told him that my dad had had a brain aneurysm when he was thirty-four, his body language immediately changed. He stood up and told Barry to take me straight to the closest hospital emergency room. "Tell them you need a CT scan with dye and you need it now!"

We drove in silence to the emergency room. Pieces of my dad's story flashed through my mind. His brain aneurysm didn't kill him, but it changed his life and the lives of our entire family overnight. The immediate impact was that he was paralyzed down one side and lost the ability to speak, but there was a far greater storm on the horizon. As days turned into weeks, his behavior began to deteriorate. He went from being a loving, kind dad to an angry, unpredictable, and ultimately violent stranger. When it was no longer safe for us to have him in our home, he was taken to our local psychiatric hospital. He managed to escape one night and took his own life, drowning in the river that runs through our town.

I've often wondered what was going on in his mind and heart in those last few minutes. Was it regret over his violence and the terror he saw in his children's eyes? Was it despair over his own profound limitations? Only God knows the answer to those questions. Whatever was happening, I know now that my dad, healed and whole, is safely home with Jesus, but as a child, seeing every day the changes that took place in him was terrifying. Growing up, I would have nightmares that the same thing that hit him like a rogue wave would hit me too. I couldn't imagine the agony of being trapped inside a body that no longer worked as it once did, and the thought of becoming a terrifying stranger to those I loved was unthinkable. Now, driving to the hospital, it felt as if that nightmare might become my reality.

When Prayer Feels Impossible

I wonder if you have been there too? The circumstances might be different, but the impact, the possibilities, are the same. What do you do when out of nowhere an unexpected wave hits you? What is your first response when your feet are knocked out from under you and you can hardly breathe? We all face such moments in life. These experiences are outside the normal day-to-day challenges. They are places we've never been before. I think of my friend whose husband has a brain tumor or the woman who stopped me recently in a coffee shop to tell me she had just come from her doctor's office and he had told her she has cancer. The shock on her face was heartbreaking. It's the look you have when you are blindsided by a piece of news that nothing could have prepared you for. One moment you're thinking about what to cook for dinner and the next you're wondering if you'll be around to cook many more dinners.

One of the most sacred things in my life is the trust many women place in me. I don't take it lightly when either in a note or face-to-face someone shares their pain and their questions. Even as I'm reading or listening, I'm lifting them up to the throne of grace and mercy and praying the promise of this text over them:

> So let us come boldly to the throne of our gracious God. There we will receive his mercy, and we will find grace to help us when we need it most. (Heb. 4:16)

We will find grace when we need it most. Sometimes our need is overwhelming.

My son is on drugs again, and I don't know where he is tonight.

My husband embezzled money from our church, and he is going to prison.

My daughter is living with a man twice her age, and I think he is abusing her.

I think my husband is a pedophile.

I had an affair, and I'm now pregnant with another man's child.

How do you pray when it feels as if your very breath has been knocked out of you, when the only sounds you can make resemble the moans of an injured animal, when prayer feels impossible? You wonder how you can even find words to wrap around what you're dealing with. Where do you start? The road ahead is pitch black—no lights, no signs to give even the smallest clue. You don't have a map for this journey. No, you don't have a map, but in Christ, you do have a guide. As the darkest days in human history began to unfold, Jesus gave us a blueprint of how to pray when it's hardest to pray.

It Begins

My soul is overwhelmed with sorrow to the point of death. (Mark 14:34 NIV)

If you read Mark's Gospel, you will see that in chapter 14, the pace picks up. It's the beginning of the end for Jesus. By the end of that chapter, Christ has been betrayed and arrested, but Mark begins by setting the stage for the final act, telling us that it's now two days before Passover and the Festival of Unleavened Bread.

Passover was one of the three great feasts for the Jews. Thousands flocked to Jerusalem to celebrate and the preparations that took place during the previous month were extensive. Roads were restored, trash was taken away, and the true meaning of Passover was taught over and over again in the temple. Burying people by the side of the road was common in those days, but no pilgrim on their way to Jerusalem could come in contact with a dead body. If they did, they would not be allowed to participate in the feast. So according to Scottish theologian William Barclay, all those wayside tombs were whitewashed so that they could be recognized and avoided.[1]

Every adult male who lived within fifteen miles of Jerusalem was required to celebrate in the city, but thousands more came from all around the world. The great irony of this story is that Jerusalem was crammed with those who came to sacrifice a lamb to God, not knowing that the perfect Lamb of God was about to be slaughtered outside the city walls.

Jesus's Blueprint for Prayer

When evening came, Jesus arrived with the Twelve. While they were reclining at the table eating, he said, "Truly I tell you, one of you will betray me—one who is eating with me."

They were saddened, and one by one they said to him, "Surely you don't mean me?"

"It is one of the Twelve," he replied, "one who dips bread into the bowl with me. The Son of Man will go just as it is written about him. But woe to that man who betrays the Son of Man! It would be better for him if he had not been born." (Mark 14:17–21 NIV)

I've often wondered how Jesus could sit and celebrate Passover with His friends, knowing what would happen in just a few short hours. They had no idea what the night would hold, but Jesus did. I used to imagine that on that evening, they reclined at the table and simply talked to one another, but I was wrong. The celebration of Passover was a very detailed, holy event, a remembrance of how God delivered His people out of Egypt. There was an order to the stories that were told, when the wine was taken, when the bread was broken. Bitter herbs were placed between unleavened bread to recall the bitterness of their ancestors' captivity. Songs of deliverance were sung, and as they left the upper room and made their way to the Mount of Olives, the disciples and Jesus sang the final song of Passover as they walked, Psalm 136:

> Give thanks to the Lord, for he is good!
>> His faithful love endures forever.
> Give thanks to the God of gods.
>> His faithful love endures forever.

Give thanks to the Lord of lords.
His faithful love endures forever. (vv. 1–3)

As they sang, they had no idea how good. They had no idea how faithful. As the clock continued to count down to His betrayal, Jesus took His friends into the olive grove called Gethsemane. There were no gardens inside Jerusalem, but some wealthy families had gardens outside the city walls. One family must have been friends of Jesus and welcomed Him to use their garden for prayer. That night, leaving eight of the disciples by the entrance, Jesus took Peter, James, and John farther into the garden to be with Him. The full extent of what was about to take place washed over Jesus in overwhelming waves. He knew what was ahead, and now it was only a few hours away. I have a hard time reading the next few verses. We are invited into the very private agony of our Savior. If you have ever asked yourself, *How do I pray in this place, this unfamiliar, devastating territory?* listen in. Jesus invites us into His own prayer.

He took Peter, James, and John with him, and he became deeply troubled and distressed. He told them, "My soul is crushed with grief to the point of death. Stay here and keep watch with me."

He went on a little farther and fell to the ground. He prayed that, if it were possible, the awful hour awaiting him might pass him by. "Abba, Father," he cried out, "everything is possible for you. Please take this cup of suffering away from me. Yet I want your will to be done, not mine." (Mark 14:33–36)

I am stunned by Christ's vulnerability and brutal honesty here. Even though He had set His feet to walk through this hell, there was no hint of bravado, no putting on a brave face. Jesus was honest, crushed with grief to the point of death. Luke, the doctor, gives us a detail that Mark's account omits. It would have been significant to a medical man.

He prayed more fervently, and he was in such agony of spirit that his sweat fell to the ground like great drops of blood. (Luke 22:44)

72

Jesus's sweat fell like great drops of blood. This condition, hematohidrosis, results in the excretion of blood through the sweat glands. I can't imagine the kind of agony that would make this possible. As a physician, Luke recorded this rare yet significant physiological phenomenon that occurs only in cases of extreme agony. Luke wanted us to know what Jesus's suffering cost Him. There have been rare cases of hematohidrosis recorded in our time, and what we now know is this: while the extent of blood loss generally is minimal, hematohidrosis results in the skin becoming extremely tender and fragile, which would have made the crucifixion even more painful.

When you are walking through the unimaginable, don't ever feel that you are required to keep your chin up and be a "good witness." The perfect Lamb of God made it crystal clear that some things are simply too hard to face, some things we can't do on our own. Jesus asked His closest friends to be with Him as He prayed. Friends can't take the pain of life away, but they can make us feel less alone. When you are in a Gethsemane of your own, you don't really want another's words, just their presence. Was that why Jesus asked His friends to watch with Him? Perhaps Jesus wanted them to stay awake as He prayed to prepare them for the violent night that lay ahead as they heard Him pray in such agony? Perhaps they were to be unwitting lookouts for the sound of marching boots and the sight of flaming torches so that Jesus could have the time He needed to talk to His Father.

Yet as Jesus fell to the ground and began to pray, it's clear who He was turning to for strength. He was not depending on His friends for strength but on His Father, His Abba. This is the only record of Jesus calling God Abba. It's such an intimate, personal way for a son to call out to his papa. The term *Abba* is found in Scripture only three times and is used once by Jesus and twice by Paul (Mark 14:36; Rom. 8:15; Gal. 4:6). Paul used this intimate term in writing to the church in Rome and the church in Galatia (central Turkey). *Abba* is an Aramaic word. If you ever take a trip to Israel, you will hear young children call to their fathers in the crowded marketplaces, "Abba," "Papa." In His agony, Jesus used the most familiar and familial term of all, *Abba*.

Some have questioned whether the agony of Christ was real. Since He is the Son of God, did He have supernatural strength for what lay ahead? Christ was fully God and fully man, and it was Christ the man who fell to the ground in the garden that night. Jesus, in His humanity, didn't want to die. He knew that although the physical pain of crucifixion would be almost unbearable, the greatest pain of all would be that moment on the cross when the sin of the world would be poured out on Him and for the only time in eternity He would be separated from His Father. Jesus prayed two critical things that we need to understand when we face our darkest days.

First, He begged for a way out. He cried out, "Everything is possible for you. Please take this cup of suffering away from me" (Mark 14:36).

I've heard the essence of that prayer from thousands of women over the years in a multitude of ways. *God, You are big enough to take this away. Nothing is impossible with You. I have faith in You. I believe You can change this. I don't want to do this. Please, please take this away. Save my marriage. Heal me. Save my child. You know You can. Please, God, I'm begging You!*

If Christ begged to be released from what lay ahead, why should we think we lack faith when we pray the same way? We get to be real with God. We are invited to come just as we are, emotions raw, heartbroken, desperate. Having wept until we have no tears left, no words left, we listen in again as Christ continues to pray.

Second, He prayed for God's will to be done. I've wept with friends as they too have bowed their broken hearts to our God, whose ways are higher than ours, whose thoughts are so far beyond our understanding. Such prayers turn a living room into holy ground. *I want my life to glorify You. I know You could change this, but if that's not Your will, I want Your will. I don't understand it, but I accept it. I love You, and if this is the way things should be, then I say yes!*

We serve a loving Father who weeps with us, who collects our tears. I love this promise in Psalm 56:8:

> You keep track of all my sorrows.
>> You have collected all my tears in your bottle.
>> You have recorded each one in your book.

Peace in the Not-Knowing

The traffic was terrible in Dallas that day as Barry drove me to the hospital. It's usually bad, but that day it seemed particularly slow. I knew he was anxious and worried as he uncharacteristically honked at the car in front of us to move. I was somewhere else. What I needed wasn't an answer; I needed Jesus. I put my seat back and closed my eyes and talked to my Abba Father.

I don't know what this is. I'm scared. If there's something in my brain that's about to burst, please stop it! I don't want to do this to my son. It would be too hard. Please help me.

Suddenly, the traffic began to move, and before I knew what was happening, Barry had pulled up outside the emergency room. We walked into a room filled with people—some with desperate looks on their faces and others waiting for answers. In one corner, a child was crying as his mother held a bloody towel around his arm. Barry told me to take a seat and went to talk to the woman at the check-in desk. I don't know what he said, but I was suddenly taken back to a room and a young doctor began to ask me questions. Everything seemed to be happening so quickly. I changed into a gown and was taken back for a CT scan within minutes. I lay flat on my back as the table went into the scanner. It was cold and hard. Things whirred around my head as I was told to lie still and not move. It looked as if I was alone in there, but I wasn't.

Here we are, Lord. This is scary. I'm so glad You're with me. So here's what I think. I'd like there to be nothing wrong, but more than that, I want Your will. I really do. You are my everything. If this thing bursts and everything changes, You'll still be with me. And You love Barry and Christian more than I ever could, so I'm letting go. I love You, Jesus.

> When you are right in the middle of the hardest days, Christ promises His presence and His peace.

When the scan was over, I was taken back to the room where Barry was, and we waited and waited. Finally, the doctor came in. He said, "Good news. Everything is fine. You might be working a bit too hard. Take a day off every now and then," and then he rushed off to the next patient.

I got dressed and we left. It was surreal. So much had happened in just a few short hours, but the greatest gift of that day was the peace Christ gave me before I knew what was going to happen. When you are right in the middle of the hardest days, Christ promises His presence and His peace.

He Likes to Be Asked

There are key moments in life that show you what has been going on in your heart and spirit even though you might not have been aware of growth or change. I'm sure you can think of a few. Something happens, and you react differently than you would have ten, twenty, or more years ago. Those moments show us how God in His mercy has strengthened us and how the Holy Spirit has been molding us. One of the greatest lessons I'm learning from the life of Christ is that prayer mattered to Him, and as we grow, it should matter more and more to us. S. D. Gordon put it this way as he summarized the life of Christ: "Thirty years of living, three years of serving, one tremendous act of dying, and two thousand years of prayer."[2]

Think about that. It is amazing.

I don't know where you are right now with prayer. If you're in a tough season that doesn't seem to be coming to an end, you may be tempted to stop praying because nothing seems to be changing. What I've learned, though, is that when I keep praying, when I refuse to give up, when I pray hardest when it's hardest to pray, I'm changed whether the circumstances change or not.

Someone asked me at a recent speaking event why we should even bother to pray if God knows everything anyway. Her reasoning was that God already knows what He's going to do, so why bother? I told her that if praying mattered to Jesus, then it should matter to us. I added that I think God likes to be asked. I'm a huge C. S. Lewis fan and have read all of his children's books. I love this dialogue from *The Magician's Nephew*:

"Well, I do think someone might have arranged about our meals," said Digory.

"I'm sure Aslan would have, if you'd asked him," said Fledge.

"Wouldn't he know without being asked?" said Polly.

"I've no doubt he would," said the Horse. "But I've a sort of idea he likes to be asked."[3]

I've sort of an idea He likes to be asked too. No matter what you are facing right now, talk to your Father. Remember Jesus's prayer in the garden on that dreadful night. Be honest. Be real. Pour your heart out. Yell if you need to, until you've said everything you need to say, and then lift your heart and hands to heaven and pray with our Savior, *Yet I want Your will to be done, not mine.* It's hard, I know. If you're in one of the most difficult places you've ever been, prayer may feel impossible. Remember our Savior. On the night when it seems that prayer would have been the hardest, it was what mattered to Him the most.

Praying women press through in prayer even when life is tough.

PRAYER REMINDERS

1. Pray hardest when it's hardest to pray.
2. Pray like Jesus, brutally honest and completely vulnerable.
3. Pray for God's will to be done.

A PRAYER WHEN IT'S HARD TO PRAY

Father,

I don't understand what's going on in my life right now. It's too hard. You are big enough to change it, You are loving enough to want to, yet nothing seems to change. I don't like this. I don't want this. I'm crying out to You for help. I want to pray as Jesus prayed, but I need Your help. I want Your will; help me to want it more. I want to surrender; help me to let go. I trust You; help me to trust You more. In Jesus's name, amen.

FIVE

Pray Through Your Pain

*Praying women pray through their heartache
until it becomes their authority.*

Although the world is full of suffering, it is also full of the overcoming of it.

Helen Keller

We are pressed on every side by troubles, but we are not crushed. We are perplexed, but not driven to despair. We are hunted down, but never abandoned by God. We get knocked down, but we are not destroyed. Through suffering, our bodies continue to share in the death of Jesus so that the life of Jesus may also be seen in our bodies.

2 Corinthians 4:8–10

We buried my mum in the summer of 2016. She was eighty-six years old. I stayed in Scotland for a few days to help my sister, Frances, sort through her things, and then I flew home to Dallas. We had talked about what we'd like to put on her headstone. She was buried in the same plot as her parents, so we chose a bigger stone to include all three. When Frances sent me a picture of the finished piece, I felt as if I had been stabbed in the heart. This was not a new wound; it was a very, very old one. The stone read in part:

> In loving memory of Alexander Nicol [my grandfather], his wife, Margaret Nicol [my grandmother], and their daughter, Elizabeth Walsh. Much loved parents and grandparents. At peace with the Lord.

It was beautiful. It was what we'd talked about, but suddenly what was missing was crystal clear, an absence in the marble. Where was my father? Why wasn't he mentioned?

My dad's violent behavior after his brain aneurysm had made him a terrifying person to be around. After he was committed to a local asylum, he managed to escape one evening and made his way back to our house. I've never talked about that evening before. I don't know all the details of what happened that night, as it was hard for Mum to talk about. Suffice it to say, there were a few terrible hours before the asylum staff arrived to take him back.

After my dad took his own life, he was buried somewhere in an unmarked grave, and we moved out of that town. He wasn't himself when he died, and I have wept many private tears throughout the years at the thought of his resting place being left unmarked, unknown. I flew home to Scotland once and tried to find his grave, but I couldn't. I know that he is home with Christ, but I grieve the shame in which he was buried. When I saw the picture of Mum's gravestone, I felt a fresh wave of pain and sorrow for my dad. Even old wounds still hurt.

How do you pray about something you can't change? How do you pray when it feels as if you don't even know how to put into words what you're asking for? All I could say was, "Lord, this hurts so badly." Perhaps one day we will find the place where he was buried and this will be resolved and we'll finally be able to raise a stone that says:

> In loving memory of Francis Walsh, husband of Elizabeth and beloved father of Frances, Sheila, and Stephen. At peace with the Lord.

Until that day, I will pray through my pain.

Purified by Pain

Pain comes in all sorts of packages. Sometimes they are deep emotional wounds. Other times the wounds are physical, almost more than you can bear.

In the spring of 2017, I interviewed my friend Michele Cushatt on my television program *Life Today*. I knew Michele before cancer, and now she sat with me in the studio after her third bout of mouth cancer.

The first came when she was just thirty-nine years old. She was told by her doctor, right before Thanksgiving, that she had squamous cell carcinoma of the tongue. She'd never even heard of such a thing. Apparently, it's something heavy smokers can face, but Michele had never touched a cigarette. What followed for her were doctors' appointments, PET scans, and a painful surgery to remove a small section of her tongue. After that first surgery, the doctors told her this was the best scenario possible. They had caught the cancer early. Then it came back. Twice. Three years later and again eight months after that. The last bout was devastating and life altering. A nine-hour operation followed by two months of chemotherapy and radiation.

As she sat in the makeup chair before we began taping, her eyes met mine, and I can't find the words to adequately express what I saw there. Was there victory? Yes, she's alive and with every breath giving the glory to God, but there was more than that. What I saw was just a glimpse of what this experience is still costing her. That's not our favorite kind of story. We'll accept the difficult beginning, then a struggle in the middle, but we want a happy ending in which the pain is in the past. That's not her story, and it may not be yours either. How do you remain a praying woman when your prayers have not been answered as you wanted them to be?

As Michele sat opposite me, I knew that talking was very difficult for her. She has only a third of her tongue left, so speech is painful, but the authority in every hard-won word was astonishing. She told me that she used to love Easter Sunday—after all, it's our glory day in the church celebrating the risen Christ. But she told me that now she finds great comfort on Good Friday as well, knowing that Christ understands her suffering. In my mind, it's no accident that the enemy tried to take away her ability to speak. She is a powerful communicator. But as always, he overplayed his slimy hand. One-third of a tongue consecrated to Christ is a more powerful weapon than a thousand tongues without Jesus. When everything we used to depend on is stripped away and we are shaken to the very core of who we are, either we walk away from faith or we are all in, totally devoted to our wounded Savior. When Michele prays now, the battle lines are very clear. There is an enemy, and there is Christ, who wears the Victor's crown. She has learned to do fierce spiritual battle on the front lines of suffering.

> *When everything we used to depend on is stripped away and we are shaken to the very core of who we are, either we walk away from faith or we are all in, totally devoted to our wounded Savior.*

Where Your Wounds Are, There Lies Your Authority

As I write, I wonder about your life and what you've been through. What are the things you never said yes to but they happened anyway? What are the losses? What are the struggles? When your eyes have shed so many tears, it clears your spiritual vision.

I've seen that happen in another friend, Darlene Zschech. So many love her for the worship song "Shout to the Lord" that she wrote when she was a worship leader at Hillsong Church in Sydney, Australia. I knew and loved Darlene back then, but after she was diagnosed with breast cancer in 2013, I got to know an even more anointed Darlene. A week before Christmas, out shopping with her husband, Mark, she popped into the Sydney Breast Clinic to get the all-clear on a tiny lump and instead was told she had cancer. She walked through a brutal year of chemotherapy and lost her lovely blonde hair, but something deep inside her shifted. We were in an arena together recently with about five thousand women, and Darlene asked them to stand if they had received a diagnosis of breast cancer. I was overwhelmed to see how many women stood. Then she began to pray. It was one of the most anointed, powerful prayers I've ever experienced. She prayed as one with authority because she'd been there. I watched her reach through the pain of her experience and pray for other women. It was truly a holy moment.

My story and the stories of Michele and Darlene are most likely different from your story. You have a story of your own, and where your wounds are, there lies your authority in Christ. We can either back down in the midst of struggles or, by God's grace, stand up and pray through the pain. Let me pause here and acknowledge how black-and-white that might sound. Life is rarely as clear-cut as that. You may be in the greatest pain of your life, and you are struggling to pray through it. As I've searched my own heart and asked the Holy Spirit for understanding, I've realized that often we struggle not because of our view of God but because of the lies we've believed about ourselves.

> *We can either back down in the midst of struggles or, by God's grace, stand up and pray through the pain.*

The Lies We've Believed

I thought and prayed about this for a long time and asked the Lord, "What are the lies I've believed?" The answer shocked me and showed me how deeply these lies can be embedded and how long we might have believed them to be true. As the Lord began to reveal the greatest lie I've believed, it was hard for me to face. It's difficult to write about.

Since I was a child, I've had a deep-seated fear that I will eventually be killed by the one who is supposed to love me most. The origin of the fear is not hard to trace. I was torn in my emotions about my father. I adored my dad, but his brain aneurysm turned him into a different person, an angry stranger one day and a weeping, repentant father the next. It was like living in the reality of Dr. Jekyll and Mr. Hyde, not knowing which one would wake up each morning. I'm pretty sure this is why I'm afraid of clowns or anyone in a mask. I remember after a concert years ago, my British band thought it would be fun to get pizza at the children's food and fun place Chuck E. Cheese. I was standing in line waiting to pay for their food when someone tapped me on the shoulder. When I turned around and saw someone in a mouse costume, I screamed and threw a tray at him. Everyone in line thought it was funny, and I pretended that I did too, but the truth is, I was terrified. Because I couldn't see the person's eyes, I didn't know which one was in front of me, the good one or the evil one.

What was shocking to me is that I've allowed my fear to remain tucked way down deep in my soul for so long, and now I've transferred my fear onto my very loving husband, Barry. If Barry is driving (he is a good driver, by the way!), I have this gut-level fear that we'll be in an accident and I'll be the only one killed. I will be able to see it coming, but there will be nothing I can do to stop it. I'm sure I felt powerless against my dad's rage when I was a little girl, but the truth is that Christ was with me then and He is with me now. I'm horrified that I've given territory to the enemy to torment me for so long. I belong to Christ. My days are in His hands. So I have renounced my fear in the powerful name of Jesus Christ. That's my prayer for you as well. As Paul wrote to the church in Corinth, although Satan is hunting us down, we are never abandoned by God (2 Cor. 4:9–11).

What are the lies you've believed? What pain have they caused in your life? What choices have they made for you? It's time to face them in Jesus's name and replace them with truth. Throughout the years, so many women have shared with me the deep-seated lies they've allowed to take root. The enemy doesn't want you to pray through your pain. He wants you to stay in it so you can never move on with Christ. Here are some of his lies. Which ones are holding you back?

I'm not enough.
I'm not worth loving.
I'm not a good wife.
I'm not a good mom.

I'll never change.

I can't do this.

I'll never get past my past.

I don't belong.

I'm always going to be alone.

I'll never be able to move on.

The number one lie that I hear more often than any other is the first one: "I'm not enough." It doesn't seem to matter whether we are rich or poor, successful in the world's eyes or not, that lie seems to be central, the most primal lie of all. I believe there's a reason for that. It was the first lie ever spoken on our planet. It's what Satan insinuated to Eve. He wanted her to believe that God was holding out on them, that as they were, they were not enough. This was our very first "not enough" moment.

"For God knows that when you eat from it your eyes will be opened, and you will be like God, knowing good and evil."
When the woman saw that the fruit of the tree was good for food and pleasing to the eye, and also desirable for gaining wisdom, she took some and ate it. She also gave some to her husband, who was with her, and he ate it. Then the eyes of both of them were opened, and they realized they were naked; so they sewed fig leaves together and made coverings for themselves. (Gen. 3:5–7 NIV)

Satan's message was clear: "As you are now, you're not enough, but if you eat of this fruit, you will be." Believing that lie devastated Adam and Eve's lives and has been messing with us all ever since. It seems to be built into our DNA. If the enemy can make us buy into that lie and the shame that comes with it, then all the other lies are easier for us to believe as well. If we feel that we have failed as a wife or a mom or whatever, it all stems from the lie in the garden that we are not enough. When we allow that to be the truth we believe, we stay stuck in shame and don't live the lives God has called us to and equipped us for. We stay stuck in our pain and can't pray through it. Satan knows the power of prayer. Jesus told us what the enemy's mission is, but He also revealed His plan—life! Not just survival but life, and life to the full.

> The thief comes only to steal and kill and destroy; I have come that they may have life, and have it to the full. (John 10:10 NIV)

Perhaps We're Not Supposed to Be Enough

There is a spiritual mystery here that's worth unpacking until it's clear. Because we live on a broken planet where sin was introduced, we will always experience feelings that life is not what it's supposed to be this side of eternity. This was not God's plan A. No marriage will ever be perfect. No parenting will be flawless. No one's sense of self-worth will ever be accurate. When we make it our quest to get to those places, that's when we feel defeated and less than. We are not supposed to be enough. That's why Jesus came.

Our Warrior Prince steps into our stories and redefines who we are, not in ourselves but in Him. When Paul wrote to the church in Galatia, he reminded them of this spiritual truth:

> My old self has been crucified with Christ. It is no longer I who live, but Christ lives in me. So I live in this earthly body by trusting in the Son of God, who loved me and gave Himself for me. (Gal. 2:20)

The believers in Galatia were being taught a different, false gospel than the one Paul had shared with them. They were now being told that if they wanted to please God, they had to adhere to Jewish laws. The church in Galatia was a Gentile church, and when Paul first visited and preached the gospel, the people received it in faith, but now they were being led astray. Paul made it clear to them and to us that there is nothing they or we can do to try to be good enough for God. Jesus did it for us. You and I live in these earthly bodies we've been given, but our trust is in Christ. On our worst day or our best day, we are loved and received the same because

Christ lives in us. The enemy would love for you to feel like an outsider, like you don't quite fit in, but you do. You're family!

When you feel as if you don't belong:

> See what great love the Father has lavished on us, that we should be called children of God! And that is what we are! (1 John 3:1 NIV)

When you feel unloved or unlovable:

> We know, dear brothers and sisters, that God loves you and has chosen you to be his own people. (1 Thess. 1:4)

When you find it hard to forgive yourself:

> He is so rich in kindness and grace that he purchased our freedom with the blood of his Son and forgave our sins. (Eph. 1:7)

When you feel alone:

> And I am convinced that nothing can ever separate us from God's love. Neither death nor life, neither angels nor demons, neither our fears for today nor our worries about tomorrow—not even the powers of hell can separate us from God's love. No power in the sky above or in the earth below—indeed, nothing in all creation will ever be able to separate us from the love of God that is revealed in Christ Jesus our Lord. (Rom. 8:38–39)

When you think you'll never make it through this life:

> And I am certain that God, who began the good work within you, will continue his work until it is finally finished on the day when Christ Jesus returns. (Phil. 1:6)

There are so many more Scripture passages I could share here, but the point is that God says we are His children, we are loved, we are forgiven, we are united with Christ, and we are being completed in Him. To be praying women who determine to pray through the pain of life, we are going to have to fight for our faith. We are going to have to choose to believe that what God says about us is true no matter how loud the lies are. It would be lovely if we just went to sleep and woke up full of faith, but Christ asks us, "Would you like to get well?" If the answer is yes, then there is a choice you and I have to make for ourselves.

Would You Like to Get Well?

I never understood the following story when I was a teenager. I thought the question Jesus asked was the strangest question He could ask someone. If a man was sick, of course he would want to get well. I see now that there is more to the story than I first understood.

> Afterward Jesus returned to Jerusalem for one of the Jewish holy days. Inside the city, near the Sheep Gate, was the pool of Bethesda, with five covered porches. Crowds of sick people—blind, lame, or paralyzed—lay on the porches. One of the men lying there had been sick for thirty-eight years. When Jesus saw him and knew he had been ill for a long time, he asked him, "Would you like to get well?"
>
> "I can't, sir," the sick man said, "for I have no one to put me into the pool when the water bubbles up. Someone else always gets there ahead of me."
>
> Jesus told him, "Stand up, pick up your mat, and walk!"
>
> Instantly, the man was healed! He rolled up his sleeping mat and began walking! (John 5:1–9)

If you have ever traveled to Israel and visited St. Anne's Church in Jerusalem, you may have seen the excavation that has revealed this ancient pool. Some say its name means "House of Mercy"; other translations say "House of Olives" or "House of Grace." Whichever one is correct, one thing is clear: it became a house of grace and mercy for a man who had been lying there since before Christ was even born. We don't know why Jesus chose this man. The porches surrounding the pool were crowded with people who were sick, blind, crippled, lame. I wonder if Jesus chose him because he seemed like the most hopeless one, having been there for so long.

The reason the porches were filled with sick people was because they believed that at certain times an angel would stir the water and the first person into the water would be healed. If that's not made clear in your Bible, it's because many of our most common translations omit verse 4 (below), as many translators doubt that verse 4 was part of the most reliable original manuscripts.

> For an angel went down at a certain time into the pool and stirred up the water; then whoever stepped in first, after the stirring of the water, was made well of whatever disease he had. (NKJV)

There may or may not have been an angel there, but One greater walked among them that day. When Jesus saw the man, He knew his story. No one had to tell Him that this man had been helpless for years, just as no one has to tell Jesus what you've been dealing with for as long as you have. He stopped by this one man and asked him that interesting question: "Would you like to get well?"

I wonder if He wanted to see if the man had given up hope. I can't imagine what it would be like to be sick for thirty-eight years, waiting and praying for a miracle. The man didn't answer Jesus's question. An answer would have been yes or no. Instead, his answer was, "I can't, sir." He couldn't even hear the question because his problem was so enormous. He was right. He couldn't get himself to the water in time, but Christ, the Living Water, had come to him. When Jesus told him to stand up, he did. I've often wondered what the other sick people thought when they saw that. Didn't they all want Jesus to heal them too? The only thing that John records for us is that the religious leaders reacted in anger to a man carrying his bed on the Sabbath. No joy in his healing, just anger that he broke the rules. There is great irony to me that in a place where so many sick people lay waiting for a miracle, no one recognized the Lamb of God who walked through the Sheep Gate.

The question Jesus asked the man is one He asks us. Do you want to get well? Sometimes we become so identified with what's wrong with us, what we've been through, that it's hard to give it up. We'd rather stay in our pain. That's a trick of the enemy to make us believe that's who we are, that what happened to us has become who we are. But it is a lie. You are not what happened to you.

For the man who lay by the pool for thirty-eight years, life was hard but simple. He was dependent on the kindness of others for food and his basic needs. Now he'd have to find a job, a new identity. He might have become used to being pitied by others. Now he'd have to find a new way to relate to people.

You may have been through something unthinkable. Others know your story. You're used to being introduced that way, and to walk away from it would almost seem to be a way of forgetting your experience ever happened. I don't think that's what Jesus is asking of us. Rather, He's telling us that we are so much more than what happened. There is familiarity in our stories, but Christ isn't finished writing them yet. There's more.

What Does It Mean to Be Well?

Over the years, I've wrestled with what it means to be "well." I have so many friends who have not been healed, but they are well. I think of my darling friend Joni Eareckson Tada. I imagine you're familiar with her story. When she was just seventeen years old, she dove into the Chesapeake Bay and broke her neck. Since then she has been a quadriplegic. She is actually paralyzed from the shoulders down. We have been friends for a long, long time. I have a letter from her sitting beside me on my desk as I write. She dropped me a note just to tell me that she enjoyed my last book. What seems unspeakable to me about the pain in Joni's life is that she is now in her second battle with cancer. One of the most bitter ironies is that although she is paralyzed, she can still feel pain. So how does this brave warrior pray through her pain after more than fifty years in a wheelchair?

She enclosed this Scripture passage for me. I know she would be happy for me to share it with you.

> How joyful are those who fear the LORD
> and delight in obeying his commands. . . .
> Such people will not be overcome by evil.
> Those who are righteous will be long remembered.
> They do not fear bad news;
> they confidently trust the LORD to care for them.
> They are confident and fearless
> and can face their foes triumphantly. (Ps. 112:1, 6–8)

Joni is not healed, but she is well! From the pain and brokenness of her life, millions have been touched. Millions have been helped as this sister of ours looks back at us through her pain and says, "It's okay. Jesus is here!" She was recently hospitalized. She wrote, "It's been quite a journey since March 27th when Ken rushed me to ER. Basically, over the many years, my chronic quadriplegia has put a strain on my heart and lungs. The good news is doctors believe that with medication and with a more efficient way of breathing, my condition can be reversed." She continued, "My assignment over the last 14 days of hospitalization was straight out of Acts 20:24: 'But life is worth nothing to me unless I use it for doing the work assigned me by the Lord Jesus—the work of telling others the Good News about God's almighty kindness and love.'"[1]

Joni prays through the pain. She finds purpose in the pain. She uses the pain to tell others about the kindness and love of God.

Only Wounded Soldiers Can Serve

As a bright seventeen-year-old about to go off to college, Joni would never have chosen to sit in the chair that she has been in now for over fifty years, yet she says that she wouldn't change a thing because of the depth of fellowship and love she knows with Christ. I can't begin to touch the pain my sister has known, but I have to tell you that in my battle with depression, with dark, dark nights and days when I prayed to be gone, I wouldn't change a moment either. We can read a Scripture passage that tells us the Lord is close to the brokenhearted, but until our hearts have been broken, we can't understand how true those words are. When we offer our pain to Christ, He can make something beautiful in our lives and in the lives of others.

I recently came across a short one-act play by Thornton Wilder called *The Angel That Troubled the Waters*. It touched me deeply. In this play, Wilder imagines a doctor, desperately troubled by bouts of depression, coming to the pool, longing to be healed. One day he sees the angel trouble the water, and as he is about to step in before any of those with more obvious sicknesses, the angel stops him and confronts him with this powerful truth: the only soldiers who can serve in Love's army are those who have been wounded. It's his very wounds that have made him such a compassionate doctor.

My dear sister, I don't know your wounds, but Jesus does. You can waste those wounds or you can see them as the place where your authority lies in Jesus's name. When you pray through your pain, you become a mighty warrior in Love's army.

Praying women pray through their heartache until it becomes their authority.

PRAYER REMINDERS

1. Pray through your pain, knowing God is with you.
2. Ask the Holy Spirit to reveal the lies you've believed and to exchange them for the truth of who God says you are.
3. Pray that Christ will use your pain to make something beautiful in the lives of others.

A PRAYER WHEN YOU'RE IN PAIN

Father,

I would not have asked for this load. At times, it feels too much to bear, but You have chosen to let this be my story. I choose now to make it Your story. I hear You say, "Rise up and walk." In Your name and in Your strength, I will. Amen.

SIX

Pray When God Seems Silent

*Praying women trust God in the silence
and the not knowing.*

It's enough to drive a man crazy; it'll break a man's faith.
It's enough to make him wonder if he's ever been sane.
When he's bleating for comfort from thy staff and thy rod
And the heaven's only answer is the silence of God.

Andrew Peterson

At noon, darkness fell across the whole land until three o'clock. At
about three o'clock, Jesus called out with a loud voice, "Eli, Eli, lema
sabachthani?" which means "My God, my God, why have you abandoned me?"

Matthew 27:45–46

It was an unthinkable tragedy. Before I heard about it on the evening news,
my friend texted me and asked me to pray. Her niece, grand-niece, three
great-grand-nephews, and one great-grand-niece had been involved in a

head-on collision with an off-duty sheriff's deputy. I had met the mom and grandma. My friend had introduced them to me at a conference. The news in her text was devastating. Both women had been killed on impact. The deputy sheriff had died at the scene as well. The four children were alive but in bad shape. They were so young—ages two, three, five, and seven. The five-year-old had been flown to the hospital with a broken back, the others taken by ambulance.

Often when tragedy strikes, the family craves privacy, but my friend has always been a prayer warrior, and she begged me to share their situation with anyone who believes in the power of prayer. I put the request on my Facebook page and fell to my knees. How do you even begin to pray in a situation like this? All I knew to do was to ask God to be with these precious children who didn't yet know that their mommy and grandma had died. I asked for mercy and healing for the children. I asked for supernatural comfort and strength for the entire family. I asked for faith, for surely faith is tested to its very core when something as senseless as this happens. When three of the children were released from the hospital, I added this piece of good news to my page and asked for continued prayers for the five-year-old. As I scrolled through so many beautiful comments from people committing to pray, I noticed a few that were hostile. One person wrote, "Why would you pray to a God who could have stopped this and didn't?" Another said, "This is typical of you Christians. When tragedy strikes, all you have to offer are your thoughts and prayers."

I thought about those two comments for a while and prayed for the people who had made them. In a way, I understood what they were saying. If you're looking from a distance at what God does or doesn't do and you don't know Him personally, don't understand His mercy, His grace, or His Son, it's easy to mock those who do in the face of tragedy. If all you see is religion and not relationship, prayer makes no sense. But I heard more than anger in their words; I heard pain. Making those kinds of intense comments to someone you've never met usually means there's a story there. Who knows what prayers went seemingly unanswered in their past? I often wonder how many people have walked away from faith because they've never been told the whole gospel. Perhaps they were led to believe that if you give your life to Jesus, everything will be smooth sailing from that point onward. At times, we are good at getting converts but not necessarily at discipling them. Yet it's not only those who claim to have no faith in God who struggle. One of the greatest challenges to a life of faith and prayer is to keep praying when it feels as if God is silent.

The Faith of a Highlander

I have a profound memory from my teenage years of one man's faithful prayers. He refused to stop praying even when it seemed as if God wasn't listening. Every Tuesday night I'd go with my mum to our church prayer meeting. Ours wasn't a very large church, so perhaps thirty or so of us met every week. One of my favorite members was a gentle older man from way up north in the Highlands. I'll call him Angus. He always wore a tweed jacket with leather elbow patches. His skin was ruddy from the cold north wind he'd endured when he used to farm up there. Every Tuesday he prayed the same prayer. He asked God for his wife's salvation. She was a lovely woman who occasionally came to our coffee mornings but never to church services. Some nights he would pray in his soft, lilting accent, and others he wouldn't be able to finish as tears poured down his rough cheeks. I wept with him on so many Tuesday nights.

He had been a pilot after giving up his farm and had retained his pilot's license. So one summer's day he flew my brother and me up to the island off the north coast of Scotland where he'd been born. He thought we would enjoy the flight up the coast, and he wanted to show us the little church, or kirk, as he called it, where he had been raised. I remember looking out the window of the small plane as we got closer and closer to the fields of sheep and wondering where the landing strip was.

"There's no landing strip!" I yelled over the noise of the propellers.

"Just watch, lass!" he yelled back. "We'll just have to let the sheep know we're coming."

Sure enough, as we flew low over one of the fields, the sheep ran for their lives and we landed safely. After tea and scones at a local tea shop, we walked up the cobbled alley to the church. The doors were open, so we went inside. The floors squeaked with stories from long ago as we walked to the front, where the sun was streaming through the lone stained glass window. It contained a picture of Jesus as the Good Shepherd carrying the lost sheep back home. We sat in the stillness for a while.

"Do you mind if I ask you a question, Angus?" I said.

"No, lass, go ahead," he said.

"Well, it's about your wife. Do you ever wonder why God hasn't answered your prayers yet?"

He was quiet and thoughtful for a moment, and then he said this: "He's never failed me yet, and I don't reckon He'll start now."

There was so much more I wanted to ask him, but the look of love and reverence on his face as he gazed up at the picture in the window silenced me. I found out from my mum later that night that Angus had been praying for his wife for over forty years.

Years later, I was home on a break from seminary when Angus died. The church was packed for his funeral. This gentle man's life had touched so many. Our pastor preached a beautiful message about Angus's long obedience in the same direction and his utter devotion to Christ. At the end of the service, as those who'd come to honor his life poured out onto the street, I noticed that his wife was still sitting in the front row, our pastor by her side. I assumed he was trying to comfort her, so I left them alone. Later that day, I discovered that he had been leading her into a relationship with Jesus. When she saw the church packed with those who loved her husband and heard the compelling message about the One who had led Angus all his days, she finally bowed and his Savior became her Savior that day too.

A lifetime is not too long to pray.

A lifetime is not too long to pray. Angus wouldn't know the impact of his prayers until two years later when his wife passed and joined him in heaven.

Who We Are Becoming in the Waiting

God's Word is full of stories of men and women who waited for years to hear from God. I think of Abram and Sarai (who became Abraham and Sarah). If you were raised in church as I was, it's easy to think that you know that story, but as I've been studying it again, I've found it to be pretty mind-blowing. When God first introduced himself to Abram, Abram was seventy-five years old and a pagan. About two thousand years before the birth of Christ, this is what God said to him:

> The LORD had said to Abram, "Leave your native country, your relatives, and your father's family, and go to the land that I will show you. I will make you into a great nation. I will bless you and make you famous, and you will be a blessing to others. I will bless those who bless you and curse those who treat you with contempt. All the families on earth will be blessed through you."
>
> So Abram departed as the LORD had instructed. (Gen. 12:1–4)

There has to be more to the story than that, don't you think? I want the longer version. Don't you wish you knew how God talked to him? It had to be quite something for Abram to pack up his wife and his nephew and all his possessions and walk away from his home in Ur (modern-day Iraq). He was leaving behind his birthright, his inheritance, to follow a God he'd just met. The land that God was promising him was fifteen hundred miles away, through Haran (modern-day Syria) and eventually all the way to Canaan (modern-day Israel), but Abram didn't know how far he would have to travel. He simply believed God, and off he went. Hundreds of miles from home, he and Sarai found themselves in a country where they couldn't speak the language, they were old, and they had no children.

Let me pause this story for a moment and ask you a question: Have you ever stepped out in faith? Perhaps those around you said you were crazy, but you believed you had heard from God, and so in faith you moved forward. Having taken that job or quit that job, having moved across the country, having joined that church—whatever it was—you expected that because you had stepped up, God would too. But things didn't work out quite the way you thought they would, and you wondered, *Did I get it wrong? Did I really hear from God, or was my family right?* God's timing is rarely on our schedule. We tend to measure our understanding of God's ways and will by the outcome we see, but God is far more interested in who we are becoming in the waiting. Abram had been told that all the nations of the earth would be blessed through him, but ten years passed and nothing happened. Now he's eighty-five and still has no children.

> *We tend to measure our understanding of God's ways and will by the outcome we see, but God is far more interested in who we are becoming in the waiting.*

Ten years isn't such a long time if you're twenty, but Abram was seventy-five when God first spoke to him, so ten years was a lot. Then God spoke to him again.

> Some time later, the Lord spoke to Abram in a vision and said to him, "Do not be afraid, Abram, for I will protect you, and your reward will be great."
>
> But Abram replied, "O Sovereign Lord, what good are all your blessings when I don't even have a son? Since you've given me no children, Eliezer of Damascus, a servant in my household, will inherit all my wealth. You have given me no descendants of my own, so one of my servants will be my heir."
>
> Then the Lord said to him, "No, your servant will not be your heir, for you will have a son of your own who will be your heir." Then the Lord took Abram outside and said to him, "Look up into the sky and count the stars if you can. That's how many descendants you will have!"
>
> And Abram believed the Lord, and the Lord counted him as righteous because of his faith. (Gen. 15:1–6)

In those days, if a wealthy man died without an heir, the head servant in his household, his right-hand man, would inherit everything. But God said, "No, you will have your own son." He took Abram outside and told him to look up at the stars and to count them if he could. It's hard for us to imagine how spectacular that would have been. We live in the Western world, where there is always a degree of light from somewhere, but in those days, with no electricity, no street lights or cars, the sight would have been spectacular.

I caught a glimpse of what Abram might have seen on a recent trip to Africa, when I was working with our team from Life Outreach International and our video crew from Jyra Films. We were in Angola visiting existing feeding projects and setting up new ones in some of the most remote villages. There are no hotels within hundreds of miles of many of our projects, so when we arrived at a village, we would ask the village chief for permission to camp there that night. One night we sat around our campfire for hours talking about what we'd seen that day and what we hoped to accomplish the following one. As the fire died down and only the smoldering embers remained, I looked up at the sky. I'd never seen anything like it. Thousands and thousands of stars and planets put on quite a show that night. I sat there in wonder, knowing that the God who was holding all of that in place was my Father. That's what Abram saw too, and he believed God.

So God spoke to Abram, revealing His plans for his life, but what about Sarai? Where was she in all of this?

Coming Up with Your Own Plan B

God's message to Abram was pretty straightforward. You will have a son of your own. But God didn't speak to Sarai. He didn't include her name in His promise to Abram, and now she was seventy-five, so she came up with her own plan. It's human nature. When we can't see how God could possibly work things out, we improvise. I feel for Sarai. Her plan B was to have Abram sleep with her maid, but the plan would ultimately hurt her, it would hurt her maid, Hagar, and it would give birth to two nations that are still at war, Palestine and Israel.

My heart aches for you too if you've found yourself in a place where you were waiting and waiting and God was doing nothing, at least nothing you could see. You wanted to be married and believed that God had promised you a husband, but time kept marching on and that infernal clock kept ticking, so you reached out for what was there. Now you wonder if you made the biggest mistake of your life.

You knew God had prepared you for this new position, but your boss passed you over again, so you said forget it and left and now you feel adrift, like you don't belong anywhere.

When we fill God's silence with plans of our own that don't work out, it's easy to feel as if we've blown it and there is no way back. That is not true! God is a Redeemer, and it's not over yet. I want you to hear that. Your life, God's plan for your life, is not over yet!

I Call You Princess

Thirteen years have passed since the birth of Hagar's son, Ishmael. That's a long time for Sarai to hear his laughter, watch him run into his mother's arms, watch her husband hold his son with pride. Thirteen years of regret. She must have felt as if this was all that life was going to hold for her. "Why did I do this? Why did I suggest that Abram sleep with my maid?" she must have asked herself over and over a thousand times. But the act was done, and there was nothing she could do about it. But God could. After thirteen years of silence, God spoke to Abram again. He was now ninety-nine.

> When Abram was ninety-nine years old, the LORD appeared to him and said, "I am El-Shaddai—'God Almighty.' Serve me faithfully and live a blameless life. . . .
>
> "This is my covenant with you: I will make you the father of a multitude of nations! What's more, I am changing your name. It will no longer be Abram. Instead, you will be called Abraham, for you will be the father of many nations." (Gen. 17:1, 4–5)

In his Chaldean heritage, his name, Abram, meant "exalted father." Now he was given a new name, Abraham, a Hebrew term meaning "father of many."

But what about Sarai? Did God see her? Had she blown it because she had come up with her own plan? No, now God spoke about her by name and changed her name in a small yet significant way.

> Then God said to Abraham, "Regarding Sarai, your wife—her name will no longer be Sarai. From now on her name will be Sarah. And I will bless her and give you a son from her! Yes, I will bless her richly, and she will become the mother of many nations. Kings of nations will be among her descendants." (Gen. 17:15–16)

Sarai meant "my princess" in the land she had come from, but now God changed her name to Sarah, "princess," a Hebrew name in a land where kings would be among her descendants. No longer was she simply Abram's princess; she was a princess in her own right under God. This was a very unusual thing for God to do. Those kinds of generational blessings from God fell on the man of the house, but God gifted Sarah with the name "mother of many nations." Don't let anyone ever tell you that God's Word is misogynistic, that God doesn't love and honor women. It's simply not true. The first human being to set eyes on the risen Christ was Mary. God loves his daughters well.

When God changed a name, it was a significant thing. You might remember a few others.

Jacob, meaning "caught by the heel" or "deceiver," became Israel, "one who had prevailed with God" or "a prince with God."

When Bathsheba gave birth to a baby boy after her marriage to King David, they named their son Solomon, but God renamed him! In one of the most intimate moments in the Old Testament, we read:

> Then David comforted Bathsheba, his wife, and slept with her. She became pregnant and gave birth to a son, and David named him Solomon. The LORD loved the child and sent word through Nathan the prophet that they should name him Jedidiah (which means "beloved of the LORD"), as the LORD had commanded. (2 Sam. 12:24–25)

How beautiful is that! The Lord loved the child. In the Old Testament, we get glimpses of the outrageous, tender love of God for us, but sin, rebellion, and disobedience still stood between us and God. When Christ took all of that upon himself on Calvary, sin was dealt with once and for all. So now you can look at yourself in the mirror on days when you don't feel so lovable and speak this over your soul: "The Lord loves this child." In case you think I'm stretching the truth or that this was meant only for Jedidiah, here are Paul's words to the believers in Thessalonica:

> For we know, brothers and sisters loved by God, that he has chosen you. (1 Thess. 1:4 NIV)

Who Are You?

I don't ever remember reading the text about God renaming Solomon. If you'd asked me what the name of David and Bathsheba's first son was, I would have said Solomon, not Jedidiah. (They had a child from their adulterous affair, but that child lived only seven days.) It seems that Solomon didn't hold on to who God said he was. The only time he is called Jedidiah is when Nathan brings his message from God. Solomon didn't use his God-given name or live in the strength of that identity. We read in 1 Kings 11:1–4:

> Now King Solomon loved many foreign women. Besides Pharaoh's daughter, he married women from Moab, Ammon, Edom, Sidon, and from among the Hittites. The LORD had clearly instructed the people of Israel, "You must not marry them, because they will turn your hearts to their gods." Yet Solomon insisted on loving them anyway. He had 700 wives of royal birth and 300 concubines. And in fact, they did turn his heart away from the LORD.
>
> In Solomon's old age, they turned his heart to worship other gods instead of being completely faithful to the LORD his God, as his father, David, had been.

There's a warning here for us. God gave Solomon a new name, a name that said, you are mine, but he did not live under that identity. God has given us a new name, daughter of the King of Kings, loved by God. Will we live under that name or another label?

Single mom

Divorced

Overweight

Unmarried

Physically challenged

Stupid

Depressed

Childless

Angry

Bitter

Forgotten

Unloved

When you identify with a particular label, you tend to act within the confines of that label, but that is not who you are. You are not any of these things. If you have placed your trust in Christ, you are a child of God.

This means that anyone who belongs to Christ has become a new person. The old life is gone; a new life has begun! (2 Cor. 5:17)

If you see yourself as unloved or overweight or any of these temporary labels, you may act according to them, and then there is little to make you lift up your head and look at the stars. But if you live under the banner "I am loved by God," then you remember who you really are, all the time, good days and bad. If I should bump into you sometime, I might just introduce myself as "Sheila, but you can call me Jedidiah."

Joseph was renamed by the apostles. They called him Barnabas, "son of encouragement." Being recognized for your gift is a lovely thing. As I get older, that's what I want. I don't want to be identified as an author or a speaker or a television host. I want to be known as a lover of Jesus and His people.

You may wonder why I haven't mentioned Saul being renamed Paul. There is a popular misconception that he went from being Saul the persecutor to Paul the apostle after his conversion. That's not accurate. Ananias refers to him as Saul after his conversion (Acts 9:17), and the Holy Spirit addresses him as Saul before he embarks on his first missionary journey (Acts 13:2). The simple truth is that Saul was his Hebrew name and Paul was his Greek name.

God Is Working in the Silence

Abram and Sarai waited for a long, long time to be renamed by God. The silence made no sense to them, but God was working all along. Abraham did indeed become the father of many nations. As a seventy-five-year-old childless man living in Ur, Abram couldn't have begun to wrap his mind around what God was going to do through his life. Even as he stood with God gazing up at the millions of stars, never in his wildest dreams could he have imagined this:

> This is a record of the ancestors of Jesus the Messiah, a descendant of David and of Abraham. (Matt. 1:1)

Or this:

> Long after Abraham, Isaac, and Jacob had died, God said, "I am the God of Abraham, the God of Isaac, and the God of Jacob." So he is the God of the living, not the dead. (Matt. 22:31–32)

Waiting in the Silence of God

If you have been waiting for a long time and God has been silent, let me ask you this: Do you still believe He loves you? When answers don't come, do you still believe He is for you? Jesus asked if He will find faith among us when He returns. Will He? Do you believe God is in control? Do you believe He has a perfect plan for your life? Do you believe His timing is perfect? Until we settle how we will wait in the silence, we will be unsettled in our lives. When we determine to trust God in the silence, our faith in who He is grows stronger. Our witness becomes more powerful. Like Angus we can say to those who wonder why we're still holding on, "He's never failed me yet!" When we choose to place our hope in God, we have been promised that this hope will not disappoint (Rom. 5:3–5).

I don't say these things dispassionately, trying to guilt you into belief. I've had to face these questions myself. I had to wrestle with this issue for a long time many years ago. There was someone who was part of my career in the early days, and when our paths separated, he threatened to destroy me. All my old childhood insecurities came rushing to the surface, and I was devastated and afraid. He had influence and I knew he would use every bit of it to shut me down, and he did. I was faced with two choices. I could be angry and bitter, talk badly about him, try to put out all the little fires he'd started, and attempt to win people back over to my side, or I could let it all go, stay quiet, and trust God. That sounds very black-and-white on the surface, but if you've ever been in that kind of place, you know it's not. There are a multitude of shades in between. In that agonizing place that felt like death, I had to decide:

Do I believe God's Word or not?
Do I believe God is in control?
Do I trust God?

I could add a hundred more questions, but the bottom line was this: Do I actually believe what I've said for years, or do I believe only when life makes sense? Day after day, I came back to this text:

Very truly I tell you, unless a kernel of wheat falls to the ground and dies, it remains only a single seed. But if it dies, it produces many seeds. (John 12:24 NIV)

I struggled to identify with this verse. This was Christ speaking about His own life and the sacrifice He was about to make for all of us. Unless He, as the seed, died, there would be no fruit, no redemption, no believers. How could I even begin to compare what I was going through to what He went through? Then I read this by Rev. T. G. Ragland, a missionary in southern India:

> If we refuse to be corns of wheat—falling into the ground, and dying; if we will neither sacrifice prospects, nor risk character, and property, and health; nor, when we are called, relinquish home, and break family ties, for Christ's sake; then we shall abide alone. But if we wish to be fruitful, we must follow our Blessed Lord Himself, by becoming a corn of wheat, and dying, then we shall bring forth much fruit.[1]

So I said yes! Sometimes the most powerful prayer can be just one word: yes. I said yes to God, yes to whatever He wanted from my life, yes to letting everything die, and it did. Instead of trying to save my career, I let it all go. I went back to seminary and buried my heart in the Word of God. Doing so saved my life.

In the Waiting

I don't know where you are in the waiting, my dear sister. Right now, I pause to pray for you. I don't know who you are, but our Father does. One of the most healing things I do in times of God's silence is to meditate on His word. These are some verses that continue to help me. I pray they'll help you too.

> LORD, I wait for you;
>> you will answer, Lord my God. (Ps. 38:15 NIV)

> In the morning, LORD, you hear my voice;
>> in the morning I lay my requests before you
>> and wait expectantly. (Ps. 5:3 NIV)

We wait in hope for the Lord;
    he is our help and our shield. (Ps. 33:20 NIV)

I'm asking God to give you the gift of faith when there's no sight.

I'm asking Him to give you hope when it feels as if it's almost gone.

I'm asking Him to give you strength and a clear sky tonight to see the stars.

Praying women trust God in the silence and the not knowing.

PRAYER REMINDERS

1. Pray through the silence, knowing God is with you.
2. Welcome what God is doing in you in the waiting.
3. Pray knowing that God is working even when you can't see His plan.

A PRAYER WHEN GOD SEEMS SILENT

Father,

I kneel now in belief and ask You to help my unbelief. Sometimes Your silence is more than I can bear. Sometimes Your silence makes me feel that You don't love me, don't see me, don't care for me. But now by faith I choose to trust that You are with me. You are my help. You are my hope. Meet me here in the silence. Let my life reflect Your faithfulness. I long to feel Your presence, but I trust that You are with me. I let go of my plan B and wait for You here. I wait for You. I wait. Amen.

SEVEN

Pray with the Power
of the Word of God

Praying women don't depend on their own
strength but on the power of God's Word.

The psalms are given us to this end, that we may learn to pray them
in the name of Jesus Christ.

Dietrich Bonhoeffer

For the word of God is alive and powerful. It is sharper than the sharp-
est two-edged sword, cutting between soul and spirit, between joint
and marrow. It exposes our innermost thoughts and desires.

Hebrews 4:12

When I was between the ages of thirteen and eighteen, my music teacher
entered me each year into the Ayrshire Music Festival. It was open to
all school students within a thirty-mile radius of our town. I was en-
rolled in four categories: classical solo, duet, light opera, and the Burns

competition (based on the writings of the Scottish poet Robert Burns set to music). For the first couple of years, I found it nerve-wracking to stand up in front of forty other students, their parents, and the judge with his horn-rimmed glasses and notebook. I would literally shake as I waited for my number to be called. The first year the judge wrote at the bottom of my evaluation, "Try and calm your nerves before you sing. At the moment you sound like a cross between a sheep and a machine gun." Harsh but true. Eventually, I got the hang of it and began to enjoy the festival.

During my final year of high school, a category was added. It had nothing to do with music, so I didn't think about competing in it until my English teacher suggested I should enter. It was called Shakespearian soliloquy. I could barely pronounce the title much less contemplate what it involved, but she was persistent. "All you have to do," she said, "is learn one speech from any of Shakespeare's plays and deliver it. You have a gift for drama." I wasn't quite sure what she meant by that, but I decided it might be fun to try. I wanted to find a female character who would be interesting to play. I looked at Juliet from *Romeo and Juliet*, but she was either beside herself with love or in the throes of dying, so I passed on her. Finally, I settled on Katherine from *Taming of the Shrew*. She was feisty and outspoken, and as a well-behaved Baptist, I thought it was time to spread my emotional wings.

On the day of the competition, I realized I'd probably bitten off more than I could chew. Some of the contestants were fabulous. I cried when Juliet breathed her last breath, four times. Finally, it was my turn. The speech I had chosen was from act 5, scene 2. Technically, Katherine had been tamed by this point and was now sweet and compliant, but I thought I'd jazz the scene up a bit.

> Fie, fie! unknit that threatening unkind brow,
> And dart not scornful glances from those eyes
> To wound thy lord, thy king, thy governor.
> It blots thy beauty as frosts do bite the meads.[1]

The passage is a lot longer than that, but I'll spare you. I started off angry and defiant, and then I moved to broken and angst filled, and by the end, I'd ad-libbed a bit, throwing in a couple of Juliet's better lines, before I took a bow and swept off the stage. Shame, shame upon thy head. When the judge took the stage, he said, "Before I announce the winners, I'd like to invite one young woman back to the platform." Yes, it was me.

"What were you thinking?" he asked. "Did you not realize that Katherine had been tamed by then?"

"Yes, sir, I did," I said.

"Then why did you play her that way? And please explain why you inserted lines from another play."

"I liked those lines," I said, beginning to sound like a sheep again.

Then he said, "The authority is in the text. When you decide to come up with your own, albeit entertaining, version, you have lost authority."

As I crawled off the stage with my sheep's tail firmly between my legs, he called after me, "It might have been wrong, but it was very funny!"

His one line stuck with me. I wrote it down: the authority is in the text.

The Authority Is in the Text

For years, I struggled with prayer for the same reasons you may have. We looked at some of those reasons in the introduction. Prayer felt repetitive, I would get easily distracted, and sometimes, honestly, I would get bored. Then some years ago, I picked up a book by Donald Whitney called *Praying the Bible*. Even though I've been in church all my life and I've been to seminary twice, I had never heard of this concept before. I understood the authority of standing on God's promises and I would commit Scripture to memory, but the idea of God's Word, particularly the Psalms, as a daily prayer book was new to me. I felt as if I'd discovered a lost treasure map. I want you to know that this discovery has been life changing for me, and if the concept is new to you, I pray it will be life changing for you as well. We're invited to pray the Word of God back to God. I began to research what others have written on this subject and found so much. I don't know how I missed it for so long.

As far back as the second century, Augustine called the Psalms a school for people learning to pray. "If the psalm prays, you pray; if it laments, you lament; if it exults, you rejoice; if it hopes, you hope; if it fears, you fear. Everything written here is a mirror for us."[2]

We're invited to pray the Word of God back to God.

Ambrose, bishop of Milan in the fourth century, referred to the Psalms as a spiritual gymnasium. "Whoever studies it deeply will find it a kind of gymnasium open for all souls to use, where the different psalms are like different exercises set out before him. In that gymnasium, in that stadium of virtue, he can choose the exercises that will train him best to win the victor's crown."[3]

One of my favorite things I read was from Athanasius, one of the most influential early church fathers. He said that whereas most of Scripture speaks *to* us, the Psalms speak *for* us, they give us a language.

> In the Psalter you learn about yourself. You find depicted in it all the movements of your soul, all its changes, its ups and downs, its failures and recoveries. Moreover, whatever your particular need or trouble, from this same book you can select a form of words to fit it, so that you do not merely hear and then pass on, but learn the way to remedy your ill. Prohibitions of evildoing are plentiful in Scripture, but only the Psalter tells you how to obey these orders and refrain from sin.[4]

What a powerful statement. The Psalms speak for us. If we struggle to pray, we have found God's prayer book. No matter what you are facing at this moment, when you pray the Psalms, you are praying with the authority of the living Word of God. As my darling friend Joni Eareckson Tada wrote:

> This is not a matter simply of divine vocabulary. It's a matter of power. When we bring God's word directly into our praying, we are bringing God's power into our praying. Hebrews 4:12 declares, "For the Word of God is living and

active. Sharper than any double-edged sword." God's word is living, and so it infuses our prayers with life and vitality. God's Word is also active, injecting energy and power into our prayer. Listen to how God described His Words to Jeremiah: "Is not my word like fire . . . and like a hammer that breaks a rock in pieces?" (Jer. 23:29). Scripture gives muscle and might to our prayers.[5]

Muscle and might to our prayers! It doesn't matter if we are nine or ninety, if we've walked with Jesus for fifty years or met Him last night, when we pray the Word of God, we are praying with power.

Bring All Your Emotions to God

One of the most powerful gifts of the Psalms is that they help us bring all our emotions to God. Whatever you are going through right now, you will find language for your soul in the Psalms. Walter Brueggemann writes, "The Psalter knows that life is dislocated. No cover-up is necessary. The Psalter is a collection over a long period of time of the eloquent, passionate songs and prayers of people who are at the desperate edge of their lives."[6]

Have you ever struggled to find words for what you're feeling when you find yourself in a desperate place? Pray the Psalms. The Psalms are brutally honest. They don't disguise our pain, and they don't hide our only hope. Perhaps if we lived and prayed like the psalmist, more people would be drawn to Jesus. We waste so much time in our culture trying to "find ourselves," searching for our grand purpose, but as Eugene Peterson wrote, "The Psalms were not prayed by people trying to understand themselves. They are not the record of people searching for the meaning of life. They were prayed by people who understood that God had everything to do with them. God, not their feelings, was the center. God, not their souls, was the issue."[7]

I don't wake up every morning longing to pray. Some mornings I'm tired and I'd rather make a cup of coffee and watch *The Price Is Right*. Some days I wake up with the dark cloud of depression hovering over me, but my new commitment to pray the Psalms has given me the very weapon I need for my best days and my worst days. Because God's Word is alive, not just words on paper, when we begin to pray the Word of God, the Spirit joins with us and our spirits catch fire.

On a hard day, I love to pray Psalm 34. David is in a really bad place. He's on the run from King Saul, who wants to kill him. He lied to a priest, and that lie is going to cost many lives. He ran to another city, hoping that the king would provide refuge, but when it becomes clear that he's not safe there either, he pretends to have lost his mind. This anointed king of Israel begins writing on the walls and drooling on himself so that the king will kick him out and not kill him. He keeps running and eventually finds a place to hide in a cave. Sometimes we forget that this great king who gave us so many of the Psalms wrote some of them from really hard places. He's all alone. Eventually, a band of outcasts will join him, but for the moment, he's completely alone. So how does he encourage himself and not give in to despair? He determines to praise God no matter what. "*I will* praise the LORD at all times." He doesn't say that he wants to, just that he will.

> I will praise the LORD at all times.
>> I will constantly speak his praises.
> I will boast only in the LORD;
>> let all who are helpless take heart.
> Come, let us tell of the LORD's greatness;
>> let us exalt his name together.
> I prayed to the LORD, and he answered me.
>> He freed me from all my fears.
> Those who look to him for help will be radiant with joy;
>> no shadow of shame will darken their faces. (Ps. 34:1–5)

I love David's honesty here. He confesses his fear and the shame that can so easily make us want to hide our faces from God. Instead, David lifts his head and looks to God, the One who has been his helper all along. If you have ever felt shamed or if you live with a core of shame, you know how it can crush your spirit and remove joy and hope. As I read this psalm over and over, I thought of a friend of mine who is fighting a battle to keep her head up. I sent her this psalm with a note telling her that I was praying for her.

Right now, she is in a helpless situation. She is alone, and she is afraid. Struggling with a disability and a family who doesn't understand her faith in God is hard. They try to shame her, so I want her to remember that those who look to Jesus for help will be radiant with joy. We can share encouraging words with one another, as we should, but there is nothing more powerful than sharing the Word of God. So my friend and I set a time to pray out loud together. She's in an apartment several states away, and I'm shut away in a motel writing, but together at our chosen time we declared the truth of these words over her life. If this is your story too, pray this psalm out loud over yourself. Don't let shame make you hang your head. Lift your head high to the One who loves you and took your shame on Himself on the cross.

Praying the Psalms

Each day now, before I do anything else, I pray one of the Psalms. As Donald Whitney writes, "God gave the Psalms to us so that we would give the Psalms back to God."[8]

Let me show you what this looks like for me. Your prayer will obviously be different from mine, but I hope this example gives you an idea and a frame of reference. This is not the right way to pray the Psalms; it's just one way. Let's use one of the better known Psalms, Psalm 23:

The Lord is my shepherd; I have all that I need.

> Lord,
> *Thank You that You are my Shepherd. Thank You that You are watching over me today and that if I get lost, You will come and find me. Thank You that in You I have everything I need. I ask that You shepherd my husband and son through this day; be close to them, Lord, and guide them.*

He lets me rest in green meadows; he leads me beside peaceful streams. He renews my strength.

> *Lord,*
>
> *Thank You that You promise rest. Help me to see those places today where You invite me to sit down beside You in the quiet and let the world rush on by. Thank You that when I wait on You, You will renew my strength. I'm tired, Lord. Teach me to wait on You in the midst of the busyness of life. I ask that for Barry and Christian too. Christian has finals coming up; help him find Your peace today.*

He guides me along right paths, bringing honor to his name.

> *That's my prayer, Lord. I want to follow You. I want to walk on the right paths. I want my life to bring honor to Your name. Thank You that You are the One who guides me; I don't have to figure everything out on my own. I pray that You'll guide Barry and Christian today. Keep their feet on the right path. Let our lives bring You honor.*

Even when I walk through the darkest valley, I will not be afraid, for you are close beside me. Your rod and your staff protect and comfort me.

> *Lord,*
>
> *I lift up my dear friends to You. They have been in this dark valley for so long. Give them Your peace today; help them not to be afraid. Protect them from thoughts that would torment them. Lord, You made his brain. You can make it new. Please touch and heal him. I pray for their sons. This is so hard for them, Father. Protect their minds and comfort their hearts.*

You prepare a feast for me in the presence of my enemies.

> *The world is getting more and more hostile, Lord, but You are good. You were the same yesterday, You are the same today, and You will be the*

same when I walk into tomorrow. Thank You for all Your blessings and gifts. Thank You that Your sacrifice on the cross promises me forgiveness, peace, and joy in You.

You honor me by anointing my head with oil. My cup overflows with blessings.

Lord,

I thank You that just as a shepherd pours oil over the heads of his sheep to heal their wounds, to keep bugs and flies away that would torment them, You anoint my head with the oil of Your Word to keep away the annoying lies of the enemy that buzz around trying to distract me. Thank You for the healing oil of Your presence.

Surely your goodness and unfailing love will pursue me all the days of my life, and I will live in the house of the LORD forever.

Father,

I didn't find You; You found me. Thank You. Thank You that You have promised to finish the work You began in me until that day when I finally see You face-to-face. Your love is unfailing. Thank You, Lord. My love will fail, but Your love never will. Thank You, Father. Amen.

Do you see how in many ways I'm praying as I normally would? I'm praying for my husband and my son, I'm praying for my friend who has a brain tumor, but I'm allowing the Word of God to direct my prayers. As you get to know the Psalms better, you will know where to turn for specific prayers, but don't be afraid to flip through them until you come to one that speaks to you at that time. In *Praying the Bible*, Donald Whitney suggests the following method. Start with the day of the month, say the twenty-first, then look at Psalm 21. If it speaks to you, stay there. If not, count thirty Psalms to Psalm 51, Psalm 81, or Psalm 111. There is no right way to do this, but I promise you there is power in praying the Word of God, even when you have come to the end of yourself.

None of Our Pain Is Wasted

The church was almost empty now, and Barry was packing up a few things before we headed back to our hotel for the night, as it was getting late. After each speaking or teaching event, I try to stay as long as possible to listen to and talk with the women who have attended. Sometimes my transparency about different struggles in my own life opens up a door for them to share, perhaps for the first time, what they've been through. I don't take this part of my life lightly. It's sacred space. As I listen, I see once again that Christ is such a wonderful Redeemer, and none of our pain is wasted.

One woman was sitting alone in the very back pew. I didn't want to assume that she was waiting to talk to me, but I didn't want to leave without asking either. I slipped into the pew and asked her if she wanted to be alone. She said, "I am alone." I asked if I might sit with her for a few moments, and she said yes. I won't share her story—but some of what she was feeling may be true for you as well. She had been going through a painful situation for a long time, and she was worn-out. One thing she said pierced my heart. I've heard it so many times. She said, "No one knows the tears I've cried." She said that she has friends who were very supportive in the beginning, but life goes on. "I can't expect them to be there forever," she said. It was the thought that no one knew the depth of her pain or the tears that flowed week after week and month after month that made her feel so alone.

There are times when I have no words. Some wounds are too deep for me to try to put words to, and the reality is that although family and friends can share the burdens we carry, there are times when we find ourselves alone. I reached into my briefcase and found what I was looking for. It had been a gift from a friend a few years back. At the time, I wasn't quite sure what it was when I opened it. The small glass bottle was a beautiful cobalt blue, about two inches tall, covered in silver filigree. I thought it might be a perfume bottle, though a very small one, but her note explained that it was actually a tear bottle she'd found in a store in Israel. I did a little research and discovered that tear bottles were common in Rome and

Egypt around the time of Christ. Mourners would collect their tears as they walked toward the graveyard to bury their loved one, a tangible indication of how much that person was loved. When they reached the burial place, the bottle was placed inside as a testament to their love. Sometimes women were even paid to follow the mourners and cry into such a vessel. Apparently, the more anguish and tears produced, the more important and valued the deceased person was perceived to be.

I placed the bottle in her hand and told her why I treasure it so much and always have it with me. It reminds me of a profound spiritual truth David wrote about in Psalm 56:8:

> You keep track of all my sorrows.
>> You have collected all my tears in your bottle.
>> You have recorded each one in your book.

Even though David was in a desperate place, he found comfort in the fact that God saw everything he was going through and caught every single tear he shed. I love David's confidence in the mercy and faithfulness of God. David knew without a doubt that Almighty God never misses a moment, a tear, or a sigh from any of His children. I encouraged my broken friend to pray through this psalm every day until it began to seep into the marrow of her bones.

You are not alone.

God sees your tears.

God captures every single one in His bottle.

He alone knows the weight of what you carry.

He will never leave you.

One of the most powerful and beautiful things about praying the Psalms is that we're joining our voices with the millions who've gone before us who've prayed through these same Psalms. In the Psalms, you can find words to express every emotion, even when you feel far away from God.

When You're Spiritually Dry

I love our staff at Life Outreach International. A few of us are in front of the camera, but so many more behind the scenes have been faithfully serving God there for years. Monday mornings are for preproduction meetings at which we review upcoming guests and talk about our next mission emphasis. On Tuesday night, we meet for dinner and then head into the studio to tape three shows. One night I asked a few of the staff members what their greatest spiritual challenge was at that moment. A couple of them said basically the same thing: "I feel dried up; nothing's as fresh as it was. I feel like I'm just going through the motions. I've asked God to help me, but I don't feel a thing." The first thing I told my friends is that this is normal. We all go through times of spiritual dryness. The greatest gift we can give ourselves and the Lord is our honesty. When I'm worn-out and I can't find the words to pray, I often turn to this psalm:

One of the most powerful and beautiful things about praying the Psalms is that we're joining our voices with the millions who've gone before us who've prayed through these same Psalms.

> As the deer longs for streams of water,
>   so I long for you, O God.
> I thirst for God, the living God.
>   When can I go and stand before him?
> Day and night I have only tears for food,
>   while my enemies continually taunt me, saying, "Where is this
>   God of yours?"
> My heart is breaking
>   as I remember how it used to be:
> I walked among the crowds of worshipers,
>   leading a great procession to the house of God,
> singing for joy and giving thanks
>   amid the sound of a great celebration!

Why am I discouraged?
> Why is my heart so sad?
I will put my hope in God!"
> I will praise him again—
> my Savior and my God! (42:1–6)

This is a brutally honest psalm. The writer's heart is breaking. He remembers days when God's presence was so close, but now he's in a desperate place of discouragement. But then he catches himself and talks to his own soul. You can almost sense him stand up when he gets to "I will put my hope in God! I will praise him again—my Savior and my God" (vv. 5–6). He is declaring this truth over himself. He is shouting it into the darkness and to the enemy, who would love for us to get so fed up that we just quit. I have prayed this psalm over and over when I was exhausted and work was piling up and I just wanted to buy a one-way ticket to Bora Bora. As I declare God's truth out loud, it lifts my spirit. It reminds me of who God is and who I am and that I'm loved. If you are discouraged, would you take a few moments to pray this psalm over yourself? Perhaps you can find a quiet place or go for a walk and declare it out loud.

Christ Prayed the Psalms

Of all the reasons to pray the Psalms, no one is greater than this: Jesus prayed the Psalms. On the cross, He cried out from Psalm 22, "My God, my God, why have you abandoned me?" (v. 1).

Crucifixion was a brutal way to die. To catch a breath, the one being crucified had to push up on the three nails, one in each wrist and one through the ankles, to take in air. After Christ cried out that first verse of Psalm 22, it's not unreasonable to believe that as He let His body fall again, He continued to silently pray through that psalm. As He breathed His last, He prayed from Psalm 31: "Into Your hand I commit my spirit" (v. 5 NKJV).

When you read through the Psalms, it's clear that Jesus is everywhere. German theologian Dietrich Bonhoeffer described the Psalms this way:

The Man Jesus Christ, to whom no affliction, no ill, no suffering is alien and who yet was the wholly innocent and righteous one, is praying in the Psalter through the mouth of his Church. The Psalter is the prayer book of Jesus Christ. . . . He prayed the Psalter and now it has become his prayer book for all time. . . . Those who pray the psalms are joining in with the prayer of Jesus Christ, their prayer reaches the ears of God. Christ has become their intercessor. [9]

Christ has become your intercessor! What power. What a promise. I hope you'll see through the quotations in this chapter that praying the Word of God has always been the way for the people of God. Even when trapped in the belly of a huge fish, Jonah prayed from the Psalms:

> I cried out to the LORD in my great trouble,
>   and he answered me.
> I called to you from the land of the dead,
>   and LORD, you heard me! (Jonah 2:2)

If you continue reading Jonah 2:3–9, you'll see that he was quoting from at least ten psalms. He had been in the Psalms gymnasium. Tucked into your Bible is a prayer book. It will bring you comfort and strength, it will help you pray with power and authority, and it will guide you when the road gets dark.

> Your word is a lamp to guide my feet
>   and a light for my path. (Ps. 119:105)

Praying women don't depend on their own strength but on the power of God's Word.

PRAYER REMINDERS

1. When you pray the Word of God, you pray with power and authority.
2. Pray the Psalms daily, knowing they were Jesus's prayer book.
3. When you pray, ask the Holy Spirit to guide you.

A PRAYER WHEN YOU'RE PRAYING WITH THE POWER OF THE WORD OF GOD

Father,

Thank You for Your Word. Thank You for the Psalms. I'll begin by praying this: "Open my eyes to see the wonderful truths in your instructions" (Ps. 119:18). That's my prayer. Open my eyes to all You have for me in Your Word. Thank You for giving me a prayer book. Holy Spirit, lead and guide me as I pray back the Word of God to the Father. Amen.

EIGHT

Pray with Your Armor On

Praying women put on the whole armor of God,
trusting in His promises.

"And now," said Aslan presently, "to business. I feel I am going to roar.
You had better put your fingers in your ears."

And they did. And Aslan stood up and when he opened his mouth
to roar his face became so terrible that they did not dare to look at it.
And they saw all the trees in front of him bend before the blast of his
roaring as grass bends in a meadow before the wind.

C. S. Lewis, *The Lion, the Witch and the Wardrobe*

A final word: Be strong in the Lord and in his mighty power. Put on
all of God's armor so that you will be able to stand firm against all
strategies of the devil.

Ephesians 6:10–11

It starts with just one or two. We've had peace all winter, and then suddenly,
like the advance team for an invading army, I spot the first mosquitoes of

summer. Dallas summers are hard enough without these little thirst pests. Our summers are brutally hot. In 2011, we had forty days in a row of over one-hundred-degree temperatures. The heat is intense, but the mosquitoes make life miserable. I get some bites each year, but mosquitoes seem to be drawn to Christian and Barry like moths to a flame. When they get bitten, the bites become huge, itchy welts.

We've tried everything to make our backyard more bearable. Before Christian went off to college, he came up with the bright idea of getting mosquito nets to drape over ourselves when we sat outside. Not only did we look ridiculous, like the ghost of Christmas past, but the nets also made drinking my morning coffee very difficult. Then we tried citronella. We had candles everywhere. When that made no difference, we got tiki torches and filled them with liquid citronella. They too did nothing, apart from smoking so badly that we could hardly breathe. I did a little online research and ordered a brand-new type of repellent. I was inspired by their advertising: "Turn it on, mosquitoes gone!" Supposedly, it would create a 110-square-foot area of protection in our yard. It sounded too good to be true, and it was. Perhaps mosquitoes in other states are repelled by the tiny whiff of smoke that emerged from the unit, but in Texas, they receive that whiff like an invitation to a party.

The time when Barry seems to get attacked the most is when we walk the dogs in the evening. He's quite a sight to see as we head out. It's still so hot, even after sunset, but he'll have his pants tucked into his socks and a sweatshirt on with the hood tied tightly around his face. He'll have two mosquito repellent bracelets on his wrists and one on each ankle. Once he added dryer sheets to his ensemble. Yes, we have become the weird neighbors. We could sell tickets for the Walshes' evening walk.

This morning we reached an all-time low. Barry ordered a pup tent for the backyard so that we can sit in it with the dogs and drink our morning coffee. So if you ever fly into Dallas, and as the plane's getting lower you look out your window and see a little blue tent in a backyard, just wave, that'll be us.

Spiritual Distractions

Like mosquitoes in summer that annoy and distract, the enemy will do whatever he can to distract us from prayer. He'll pester us with thoughts, accusations, busyness—anything to keep us from our most powerful weapon. One of the most tempting distractions to overcome is relying on how we *feel* when we pray. Our feelings are never an indication of the power of our prayers, but often if we don't feel heard, we're temped to quit. The enemy would love nothing more than that. In his marvelous little book *The Screwtape Letters*, C. S. Lewis addresses this matter. The book consists of thirty-one letters written by a devil named Screwtape to his young nephew, Wormwood, instructing him on how to attack the faith of the man he is assigned to torment. One of his greatest strategies is to attack how the man prays.

> The simplest is to turn their gaze away from Him towards themselves. Keep them watching their own minds and trying to produce feelings there by the action of their own wills. When they meant to ask Him for charity, let them, instead, start trying to manufacture charitable feelings for themselves and not notice that this is what they are doing. When they meant to pray for courage, let them really be trying to feel brave. When they say they are praying for forgiveness, let them be trying to feel forgiven. Teach them to estimate the value of each prayer by their success in producing the desired feeling.[1]

As a young believer, I often fell into that trap. When I didn't feel as if my prayers went higher than the bedroom ceiling, I would get discouraged and quit praying. Not anymore. There is a spiritual battle raging all around us every day, and we're going to learn how to do battle in Jesus's name. Together we're going to move beyond our feelings. Jesus is worth so much more than daughters who only pray when they feel like it. We want our lives to count. We want to know how to pray. We want to know what to say. A very important piece of the puzzle of how to pray with authority is tucked into the prayer we call the Lord's Prayer. In reality, it's the disciples' prayer that Christ taught them in response to their question. If you've ever asked yourself, *How would Jesus want me to pray?* know that Luke and Matthew recorded the answer for us.

Teach Us to Pray

> Once Jesus was in a certain place praying. As he finished, one of his disciples came to him and said, "Lord, teach us to pray, just as John taught his disciples." (Luke 11:1)

Watching the way Jesus lived and the miraculous things He did must have made the disciples want to know why He was so different from all the religious leaders they'd ever listened to. He spoke as One who had authority. They watched how Jesus spent time alone in prayer, and so wanting to be like Him, they asked Him to teach them how to pray. Matthew places this prayer in the context of the Sermon on the Mount (Matt. 6), but Luke makes it clear that this is the prayer given to us in response to a direct question from a disciple. This is not a prayer for just anyone who wants to shoot up a few quick words to heaven; this is a prayer for those who own the name of Jesus. This is a specific prayer for followers of Christ.

> This, then, is how you should pray:
> "Our Father in heaven,
>   hallowed be your name,
>   your kingdom come,
>   your will be done,
>   on earth as it is in heaven.
>   Give us today our daily bread.
>   And forgive us our debts,
>   as we also have forgiven our debtors.
>   And lead us not into temptation,
>   but deliver us from the evil one." (Matt. 6:9–13 NIV)

The prayer begins, "Our Father in heaven." This is such a personal open door into God's presence. Addressing God as Abba would have been almost unheard of in first-century Judaism, but that is your privilege when you belong to Him. You are not going to a God you have no relationship with; you are going to your Father. If you had a good relationship with your dad, this might be an easy concept to understand. If you had or have a broken relationship with your father, it might be more challenging. Perhaps your father was critical, and you never felt you measured up. Perhaps you were not the favorite in the family. Now you are. You are the one Jesus loves. You are welcomed by your Father. I love the way Simone Weil clarifies this: "We do not have to search for him, we only have to change the direction in which we are looking."[2]

We move from that place of relationship to worship. "Hallowed be your name" is not the kind of language we would use in conversation, but Jesus is setting two things that should be diametrically opposed right next to each other: God is our Abba; He is also holy. There is no one in heaven or on earth who can compare to our God. It's easy to get blasé in prayer, but even though we are welcomed to come as we are, we must remember who God is. God is a holy God. When Isaiah saw the Lord, he thought his life was over.

It was in the year King Uzziah died that I saw the Lord. He was sitting on a lofty throne, and the train of his robe filled the Temple. Attending him were mighty seraphim, each having six wings. With two wings they covered their faces, with two they covered their feet, and with two they flew. They were calling out to each other,

"Holy, holy, holy is the LORD of Heaven's Armies!
The whole earth is filled with his glory!"

Their voices shook the Temple to its foundations, and the entire building was filled with smoke.

Then I said, "It's all over! I am doomed, for I am a sinful man. I have filthy lips, and I live among a people with filthy lips. Yet I have seen the King, the LORD of Heaven's Armies." (Isa. 6:1–5)

When we understand the perfect holiness of God, it makes the welcome to call Him Abba even more amazing. I never want to take that for granted. I never want to be so buddy-buddy with God that I lose a reverent fear and awe of who He is. At this moment, He is on the throne, holding all of eternity in place, sovereign forever.

"Your kingdom come." Have you ever been so desperate for a drink that you thought you wouldn't survive without one? I forgot to fill my water bottle once on a mission trip in Thailand. We had driven high into the mountains, hour after hour, and the temperature was over one hundred degrees. Water was all I could think about. That's how I believe Christ wants us to pray, to long for the kingdom of God on this earth. We pray for an outpouring of God's Spirit. We are the carriers of God's kingdom, and that should make a difference. When we walk into a room, the atmosphere should shift because of Who lives in us. We also pray and long for that glorious day when Christ returns and all our earthly struggles are over when we finally see Him face-to-face.

Then we pray, "Your will be done, on earth as it is in heaven." Even as we see the days getting darker, we continue to faithfully pray for the will of God to be done. We are called to pray for our nation, whether we live in America, Australia, Brazil, Scotland, or Israel. The people of God are called to pray for their nation and for their leaders that the will of God will be carried out. When Paul wrote to Timothy, he said:

> I urge you, first of all, to pray for all people. Ask God to help them; intercede on their behalf, and give thanks for them. Pray this way for kings and all who are in authority so that we can live peaceful and quiet lives marked by godliness and dignity. This is good and pleases God our Savior, who wants everyone to be saved and to understand the truth. (1 Tim. 2:1–4)

It's easy to forget to pray for those in authority. It's much easier to criticize them, but as God's daughters, we are called to pray for them. Who knows what God accomplishes in the unseen world when we align ourselves with His Word and pray.

But we don't simply look outward; we also look inward. We pray for God's will to be done not only in the life of our nation but also in our own lives and the lives of those we love. Christ prayed this way when He was overwhelmed with grief in the Garden of Gethsemane. So we too, when faced with whatever we're faced with today or tomorrow, pray not just to be spared but for the will of God to be done. I remember one of my own "Your will be done" prayers.

When after a routine physical my doctor caught what she believed to be cancer in one of my ovaries, she called to schedule surgery right away. I was actually shooting a video Bible study when I got her call. It was on a Thursday afternoon. Surgery was scheduled for Monday morning. I got up early before the rest of the crew on Friday morning and took my cup of coffee out onto the porch of the ranch where we were staying. As the sun began to rise over the lake, I left the porch and walked to the edge of the lake. I got down on my knees, and with my hands raised toward heaven, I prayed.

Father,

This is a surprise to me, but it's not a surprise to You. Thank You that You are with me right now and will be with me and the surgeon on Monday morning. This is my prayer. I want whatever will bring You more glory. If it will bring You more glory for this to be cancer—perhaps there will be someone in the bed next to me who doesn't know You—then I'm all in. I say yes! If it's Your will that this is not cancer, then thank You. Either way, my earnest plea is that You will do what brings the most glory to Your name. Because of Jesus, amen.

The results showed it was a benign tumor. I'm not sharing this as a "look at how surrendered I was" moment. No, this is me writing to you as your big sister. I gave my life to Christ at eleven and have had many, many years of experiencing the faithfulness and goodness of God. He has a track record with me. I get it, as deep as the marrow in my bones, that God is good, He is for us, He is faithful. I want you to have that confidence too so that you can say yes to God and rest in His peace.

Next, we acknowledge that we are completely dependent on God to provide for us. "Give us today our daily bread." I've been in seasons when I had a lot and seasons when I had nothing. I've gone from an expensive home to a small apartment with two white plastic chairs. What remained true in both places was that the One who is my Provider is God.

I don't know where you are financially. You may be in a great place where money is never a worry for you, or you may be in a vulnerable place where you just get by each month. I know how hard that can be. I learned more about the goodness and faithfulness of God during the days when I wasn't sure where my next check was coming from.

I'm sure those who listened to Jesus teach that day thought of their ancestors who had wandered in the wilderness for forty years. God provided food for them each day. If they tried to store it for the next day, it went bad. God was teaching them, "I'm your Provider. I am today, and I will be tomorrow." In every situation, one thing remained true for them, and it's true for us: God is our Provider, whether we have a little or a lot.

Then Jesus comes to the part in the prayer that changes everything: "And forgive us our debts, as we also have forgiven our debtors." Everything else in the prayer is focused on God, but here the spotlight turns to us for a moment. Forgiveness. Forgiveness is a game changer. If we want to know the power of God in prayer, we must forgive. It's significant that forgiveness is the only thing Jesus asks of us here. Everything else He took care of on the cross. In Matthew's account, Jesus goes on to say:If you forgive those who sin against you, your heavenly Father will forgive you. But if you refuse to forgive others, your Father will not forgive your sins. (6:14–15)

That's a very sobering statement. If we want to be forgiven, we must forgive. Who knows what revival is being held up because of a lack of forgiveness. I know that forgiving someone can be very difficult. Some atrocities carried out on this earth are unforgiveable—apart from Christ. I have a friend who was so badly beaten up by her husband that he broke her jaw. I have a friend who was sexually abused for years by her own father. How are they supposed to forgive these heinous acts? We want life to be fair, but it's not. Forgiveness is God's gift to us in a world that's not fair.

There is nothing fair about Christ's brutal execution on the cross, but His sacrifice made it possible for us to be forgiven. The innocent One took on our guilt so that we could be free and free to choose to forgive. When we choose by an act of our will to forgive, we are not excusing for a moment what happened. We are simply handing the offense over to Christ. If there is someone in your life right now whom you can't forgive, the enemy would love for you to stay that way. As long as you hold on to that weight, he can torment you with it. But Satan has nothing in his arsenal to combat forgiveness. It renders him powerless. Would you pray with me right now and give that burden to Jesus?

> *If we want to know the power of God in prayer, we must forgive.*

Father,

> *Right now, by an act of my will and not my feelings, I choose to forgive (name the person). I have held on to this for long enough, and now I want to be free. So I lay this weight at Your feet, and I will not pick it up again. If the enemy brings it to mind again, I ask You to help me lay it down immediately. I am no longer a victim. Because of You, Jesus, I am a victor! In Jesus's name, amen.*

If you have to pray that same prayer a hundred times until you are free, pray it a hundred times. The past is gone; you are a new woman. Your history will never determine your destiny in Jesus.

Finally, we ask God for His protection from the evil one. "And lead us not into temptation, but deliver us from the evil one." We are in a battle. We have a real enemy. He's not God, but he is cunning, and he hates everything God loves (that's you and me). Thanks be to God we have not been left defenseless.

A final word: Be strong in the Lord and in his mighty power. Put on all of God's armor so that you will be able to stand firm against all strategies of the devil. For we are not fighting against flesh-and-blood enemies, but against evil rulers and authorities of the unseen world, against mighty powers in this dark world, and against evil spirits in the heavenly places. (Eph. 6:10–12)

It's Time to Suit Up

Preparing for spiritual battle is critical. We don't want to engage with the enemy when we are unprepared.

One of the things I learned very early on with mission trips is that you need to dress appropriately, especially in Africa. The temperatures are often in the hundreds, so you need light cotton clothing, but you also need strong leather boots that you can tuck your pants into so that you don't get large bugs, poisonous frogs, or snakes up your pants. If what we wear for our travels matters, what we wear for everyday spiritual battles matters a million times more.

Maybe you have heard your fair share of messages on the armor of God, but my question is this: Do you suit up every day? I didn't always remember to, but I've changed that. Our world is getting increasingly evil. Our Christian faith is going to be under attack in more and more arenas, and as the day of Christ's return gets closer, our enemy will ramp up his evil. Prayer and the Word of God are our weapons.

> God's Word is an indispensable weapon. In the same way, prayer is essential in this ongoing warfare. Pray hard and long. Pray for your brothers and sisters. Keep your eyes open. Keep each other's spirits up so that no one falls behind or drops out. (Eph. 6:17–18 Message)

Before we look at the specific pieces of spiritual armor and what they mean, I want to remind you of two things the enemy is and two really important things he is not.

Satan Is a Roaring Lion

> Stay alert! Watch out for your great enemy, the devil. He prowls around like a roaring lion, looking for someone to devour. (1 Pet. 5:8)

Peter makes it clear that the enemy's mission is to take out as many believers as possible, so we need to stay alert. That's why it's so important to be in community with other believers, to be part of a local church. When you're on your own, it's much easier to drift away and get picked off, discouraged, and even pulled away from the faith. I've talked to many young women who are disillusioned with the church and think they don't need it. I understand that we are an imperfect body, but the writer to the Hebrews said this:

> And let us not neglect our meeting together, as some people do, but encourage one another, especially now that the day of his return is drawing near. (10:25)

If the day of Christ's return was close when this letter was written, it's much closer now. There are many Saturday nights or early Sunday mornings when I get home from speaking and all I want to do is crawl into bed and take a nap. But when I drag my weary self to church and we begin to raise our voices in worship together, something shifts inside me. I remember the goodness of God and how worthy He is to be praised—when we're fresh and when we're frazzled. It's much easier for the enemy to pick us off when we decide that we'll just love Jesus on our own. I understand that temptation, but it's not wise or scriptural. We need one another.

Satan Is a Liar and the Father of Lies

Jesus, talking to the crowds, described Satan this way:

> He was a murderer from the beginning. He has always hated the truth, because there is no truth in him. When he lies, it is consistent with his character; for he is a liar and the father of lies. (John 8:44)

We can go right back to chapter 3 of Genesis and see the way Satan lied to Adam and Eve, causing them to doubt the goodness of God. In Genesis 2, God warned them what would happen if they ate from one tree in the garden:

But the Lord God warned him, "You may freely eat the fruit of every tree in the garden—except the tree of the knowledge of good and evil. If you eat its fruit, you are sure to die." (vv. 16–17)

When Satan stepped in, he directly contradicted the Word of God:

"You won't die!" the serpent replied to the woman. "God knows that your eyes will be opened as soon as you eat it, and you will be like God, knowing both good and evil." (3:4–5)

Adam and Eve were never supposed to die at all but were to live with God in Paradise, eating from the Tree of Life forever, as we all were. Once they sinned, God had to put them out of the garden. They were now broken and full of shame. If they had been allowed to stay in the garden and eat of the Tree of Life, they would have lived forever, but forever broken. God loved them and us too much for that to happen.

Satan was a liar then and he's a liar now, so when you hear that old familiar voice saying, "You'll never change. God doesn't love you. No one's listening to your prayers," recognize who is talking. It's not God; it's the enemy.

So now there is no condemnation for those who belong to Christ Jesus. (Rom. 8:1)

There is no condemnation for those of us who have accepted Christ as our Savior, so when you feel condemned, know that those feelings come from the liar. He has some power, but it's very limited. What matters more is what he is not.

Satan Is Not Omnipresent

God is omnipresent, which means He's right here with me as I write and right there with you as you read. In Psalm 139, David made it clear that there's nowhere we can go from God's Spirit. You are never alone. God is always with you. Satan, the fallen angel, is not. He can be in only one place at a time, but he has his demons.

> For we are not fighting against flesh-and-blood enemies, but against evil rulers and authorities of the unseen world, against mighty powers in this dark world, and against evil spirits in the heavenly places. (Eph. 6:12)

We know from the book of Job (1:6–12) and also from Christ being led *by the Spirit* into the wilderness to be tested by the devil (Luke 4:1–2) that Satan has to get permission from God before he is allowed to touch any of God's children. I heard someone make a statement that Satan is the opposite of God. That is not true. Satan is a creature. He was created by God, as were all the angels. He doesn't hold a candle to the power of our Father. Not only is God omnipresent and Satan is not, but God is also omniscient. He knows everything, but all the enemy can do is guess.

Satan Is Not Omniscient

The fact that Satan is not omniscient is a truth we sometimes forget. Yes, Satan can lie to us, hoping we'll believe, but he has no idea whether we'll believe him or not. Let me give you an illustration of what this looks like.

Imagine yourself standing at the top of a staircase leading down into a cellar. You're feeling down, and Satan throws the first lie: "Your life will never be any better than it is right now." If you believe that, you're one step down. Then the next: "It doesn't seem as if God is listening to your prayers, does it?" Buy into that lie, and you're one step farther down. "God doesn't love you as much as he loves your friend." Another step down. He's telling you these lies hoping you'll believe him. If you accept his lies, before you know it, you're at the bottom of the cellar steps. We must combat Satan's lies with God's truth.

> "For I know the plans I have for you," says the LORD. "They are plans for good and not for disaster, to give you a future and a hope." (Jer. 29:11)

143

> Morning, noon, and night I cry out in my distress,
> and the LORD hears my voice. (Ps. 55:17)

And I am convinced that nothing can ever separate us from God's love. Neither death nor life, neither angels nor demons, neither our fears for today nor our worries about tomorrow—not even the powers of hell can separate us from God's love. No power in the sky above or in the earth below—indeed, nothing in all creation will ever be able to separate us from the love of God that is revealed in Christ Jesus our Lord. (Rom. 8:38–39)

When we combat every one of Satan's lies with the truth of God's Word, Satan has to leave.

The Whole Armor of God

Paul wrote the Letter to the Ephesians when he was imprisoned in Rome. It's one of four letters called the Prison Epistles (the others are Philippians, Colossians, and Philemon). In the first chapter of Philippians, he talks about the way God is using his imprisonment to impact the palace guards. As Paul wrote, he was literally chained to a Roman soldier. From that place with that visual beside him every day, he wrote about the armor of God.

Therefore put on the full armor of God, so that when the day of evil comes, you may be able to stand your ground, and after you have done everything, to stand. Stand firm then, with the belt of truth buckled around your waist, with the breastplate of righteousness in place, and with your feet fitted with the readiness that comes from the gospel of peace. In addition to all this, take up the shield of faith, with which you can extinguish all the flaming arrows of the evil one. Take the helmet of salvation and the sword of the Spirit, which is the word of God. (Eph. 6:13–17, NIV)

There is a powerful promise within these instructions. When we suit up every day in the whole armor of God, we will be able to resist the enemy, and after the battles we face, we will still be standing. That's a promise, but the instructions are clear: we must put on the whole armor of God, not just one or two of our favorite pieces. The more committed you are to being a praying woman, the more you will realize that you are in a battle. When you don't pay much attention to prayer or the Word of God, the enemy won't pay much attention to you, but when you've decided that you are all in, the war is on.

The Belt of Truth

On a Roman soldier's uniform, the belt was a key piece of armor. It held the breastplate on and protected a soldier's most vulnerable areas beneath his chest, his stomach, and groin. This girdle or waist belt also held his sword to his side. Without this part of his armor, the soldier could not hold on to his breastplate or his sword. Paul is telling us that without the truth of God's Word, we are vulnerable to attack. Only God's truth can defeat the enemy's lies.

The Breastplate of Righteousness

The breastplate of a soldier covered his heart. We are covered by the righteousness of Christ. When the enemy wants to attack and accuse us, we remember whose we are.

God made him who had no sin to be sin for us, so that in him we might become the righteousness of God. (2 Cor. 5:21 NIV)

It's hard for us to accept that truth. We know our failures and the number of times we've fallen down, but because of the finished work of Christ, when God looks at us, He sees Jesus. We are covered by the blood of Christ. So we protect our hearts, knowing what it cost Christ to save us. That love makes us want to live in a way that honors Him.

The Shoes of Peace

Paul saw the shoes the Roman soldiers wore to keep them steady in battle and encourages us to be steady because of the peace we have in

Christ. When we stand steady in Christ, knowing what He did for us, we are prepared to take the good news of Jesus to a world that has lost its footing. When we exhibit peace in the midst of difficult circumstances, others will want to know what we know. His name is Jesus.

The Shield of Faith

The shield that a Roman soldier used in battle was an impressive sight. It was large and oval shaped, four feet tall by two and a half feet wide, and it let nothing through. This is what we are called to hold up when life is hard. We stand strong and say, "I believe." Hebrews 11, the great faith chapter of the New Testament, begins this way:

> Now faith is confidence in what we hope for and assurance about what we do not see. (NIV)

You and I will go through tough things that make no sense, but faith allows us to worship in the darkness, knowing that God is good.

The Helmet of Salvation

The helmet covered and protected a soldier's head. The enemy would love to attack our thoughts and our minds to make us doubt our own salvation, but we can know that we belong to Christ. These are Jesus's words:

> I give them eternal life, and they will never perish. No one can snatch them away from me. (John 10:28)

I believe that this is an area that many of us struggle with as women. We play the same old tapes over and over in our minds. When I find myself falling into that trap again I stand on this verse, declaring it over my life.

> We demolish arguments and every pretension that sets itself up against the knowledge of God, and we take captive every thought to make it obedient to Christ. (2 Cor. 10:5, NIV)

The Sword of the Spirit

This final piece of armor was a surprise to me when I first studied it. I thought I understood that Paul was simply saying that God's Word is our sword in battle, but it's much more specific than that.

And take the sword of the Spirit, which is the word of God. (Eph. 6:17)

The word used for sword here is the Greek word *machaira*. It's not the word for a normal Roman long sword. This is the word for a short sword or dagger. In other words, something you would use for close combat. You'll notice too that "word of God" is with a small *w*. This is very significant. The Greek word is *rhema*, which means "a phrase or saying," not *logos*, which would have a capital *W* and is the word used for Christ, the Word, or for the whole of Scripture. What this means is that you and I can find specific promises of God in Scripture to combat the enemy's attacks on our lives. We get to customize our own weapons.

If you struggle with anxiety, find your weapon.

> You will keep in perfect peace
>> all who trust in you,
>> all whose thoughts are fixed on you! (Isa. 26:3)

Don't worry about anything; instead, pray about everything. Tell God what you need, and thank him for all he has done. (Phil. 4:6)

If you struggle with shame, find your weapon.

> Those who look to him for help will be radiant with joy;
>> no shadow of shame will darken their faces. (Ps. 34:5)

As Scripture says, "Anyone who believes in him will never be put to shame." (Rom. 10:11 NIV)

If you struggle with fear, find your weapon.

Do not be afraid, for I have ransomed you.
> I have called you by name; you are mine. (Isa. 43:1)

Don't be afraid, for I am with you.
> Don't be discouraged, for I am your God.

I will strengthen you and help you.
> I will hold you up with my victorious right hand. (Isa. 41:10)

Whatever you struggle with, find your weapon, and then as Paul writes, "After the battle you will still be standing firm" (Eph. 6:13). What a promise to every praying woman!

You don't stand alone. We stand together. One thing that Roman soldiers were known for was that they stood their ground, they didn't retreat, and they didn't break rank. Because of that, they could face and defeat any enemy. In Jesus's name, so can we!

Praying women put on the whole armor of God, trusting in His promises.

PRAYER REMINDERS

1. Pray to forgive quickly as the Holy Spirit guides you.
2. Pray as you put on each piece of the whole armor of God.
3. Pray for God's help to personalize Scriptures that become your weapons to combat the lies of the enemy.

A PRAYER WHEN YOU'RE PRAYING
   ## WITH YOUR ARMOR ON

Father,

Today I claim victory over the enemy by putting on the whole armor of God. I put on the belt of truth, standing on Your truth alone. I put on the breastplate of righteousness, remembering that I am clothed in the righteousness of Christ. I put on the shoes of peace, and today I will walk in Your peace. May Your peace radiate from me to others. I hold up the shield of faith against every lie the enemy would fire at me. I thank You for the helmet of salvation. I am Yours, and no one and nothing can snatch me from Your hand. Thank You for the specific daggers You have given me in Your Word to combat the enemy. As a praying woman, I stand strong in You. Amen.

NINE

Pray When You Need a Breakthrough

Praying women know that the greatest breakthrough is in their own hearts.

So if you're praying for a breakthrough and not seeing it, and in fact experiencing more temptations to discouragement, frustration, weariness, doubt, and cynicism than before, do not give up. Increasingly intense fighting always precedes strategic breakthroughs.

Jon Bloom

For though we live in the world, we do not wage war as the world does. The weapons we fight with are not the weapons of the world. On the contrary, they have divine power to demolish strongholds.

2 Corinthians 10:3–4 NIV

I am not a fan of early morning flights. I tend to look better after lunch. A 6:00 a.m. departure means a 4:00 a.m. wake-up call, but every now and then, it's my only option. I mostly travel on weekends, unless it's an international trip, but on this particular occasion, I had four events back to back in four different states over six days. The first event was on a Wednesday in Peoria. Everything went well there. Eight hundred women packed themselves into a university chapel as I taught on one of my favorite subjects "Celebrate your scars as tattoos of triumph." I had no idea how many little "scars" would be added as the trip progressed!

The following morning Barry and I had another 6:00 a.m. flight, this time to Chicago. The morning started as well as could be expected at gate B in the Peoria airport. It's a very small airport with no significant coffee. They had a pot of something, but it smelled like a combination of coffee, tea, and beef stew, so I passed. Boarding time came and went, and we were all still sitting at the gate wondering what was going on. I could see our plane on the tarmac, but nothing was happening. Thirty minutes later, the pilot came out and announced over the loudspeaker, "There's a bird in the cockpit!" Apparently, it had flown in when they had opened the door to begin boarding. I've heard of birds hitting planes on the outside causing a lot of damage but never of one hitching a ride to Chicago. The pilot asked if anyone had any bread to spare. I rarely carry bread, but an elderly woman behind me offered up part of her breakfast sandwich, which he took. I assumed it was to coax the bird out, but one never knows.

An hour later, he came back out without the bird or the sandwich. "It's gone into the control panel," he said. "We'll have to wait for maintenance." Maintenance eventually showed up and disappeared into the plane. Thirty minutes later, the jubilant maintenance man emerged, and we boarded the flight. We taxied out onto the runway, and the pilot announced that we were number one for takeoff. (We were the only plane.) A couple minutes later, however, he was back on the PA system: "The bird's back!" And so were we—back at the gate. We all piled off the plane again. By this time, the coffee/tea/stew brew was starting to sound good. The pilot said that the maintenance man thought he'd gotten the bird, but it must have been hiding. I'm not quite sure how you can think you've gotten a bird if you're clearly bird-less. So now he and the copilot were going to drive the plane around the airport to see if the bird would pop its head out again when it heard the engines.

You can't make this stuff up.

I watched out the terminal window as indeed they drove round and round and round. I knew by now that Barry and I had missed our connection in Chicago, but fortunately the next conference in Rochester didn't begin until the following evening. When we saw the plane arriving back at our gate, we dared to hope. The pilot announced that the bird was a "tricky little fella" and was still tucked in good and proper. I asked him what the official bird-in-cockpit protocol was. If it was just a wee bird, could we go? He assured me that we could not. The pilot and the copilot could fly the plane but not with passengers. So the three of them, the pilot, the copilot, and the bird, left for Chicago. I kid you not! I felt like breaking through the door and offering to babysit the bird, but I doubted the FAA would approve.

We had now been there for eight hours. As there were no other flights until the 6:00 a.m. flight the following morning, Barry and I found a hotel by the airport for the night. I was tired and was resting my head on my hand on the desk in our room, waiting for Barry to take his shower, when my head fell off my hand and hit the edge of the desk. I could tell immediately that one of my teeth had fallen out, as it was rolling around on my tongue. I just hoped it wasn't a front tooth, but of course it was. Right bang in the middle. How can one veneer make such a difference! I'd gone from a fairly normal-looking person to a country bumpkin in ten seconds flat. Just one little brown stump standing alone. Not only that, but I discovered that I now whistled when I talked. Barry did a little research and found out that every dentist in Rochester takes Friday off and even if there had been one who was a workaholic, there was a dental convention in Minneapolis that weekend and all were attending.

The next day our flight took off on time, and as we landed in Rochester, it began to snow. Barry asked, "Where's your jacket?"

"I guess I left it in Peoria," I said. I stepped out into the snow. "Look, Barry!" I yelled. "I'm a disaster. My hair is soaked, I don't have a jacket, and I'm toothless!" How was I supposed to get up on a platform that night? As funny as the visual was, I needed a breakthrough in my spirit to let it all go. I had to ask God to help me see beyond the things that were not working well to the whole point of my being there that night for the women who were attending. The irony was, I was speaking from my last book, *It's Okay Not to Be Okay.* I was clearly the show-and-tell, as there was very little okay about how I looked.

Days like that are frustrating, but we get through them. But there are times in life when everything goes wrong and we desperately need a big breakthrough. You may be struggling right now to hold on to your marriage with everything you've got. Perhaps you have a child who has wandered away from their faith or a child who's addicted to drugs. Or perhaps it's your own health that concerns you. You've been given a diagnosis that feels overwhelming. Whatever you are facing, one thing is clear: you need a breakthrough from God.

What Is a Breakthrough?

Merriam-Webster's dictionary defines breakthrough this way: "an act or instance of moving through or beyond an obstacle." It also means "a sudden, dramatic, and important advance." Have you ever been in a place where that was exactly what you needed? You needed a way through what was in front of you, for all you could see was a wall.

We've looked at being relentless in our prayers, faithful to keep on praying even when it feels as if God is silent. We've talked about facing each day in the whole armor of God, ready to do battle. But this is something else. How do we pray when we need a breakthrough, and what's the difference between spiritual warfare and praying for a breakthrough?

In spiritual warfare, we are suiting up to hold back the forces of darkness. We are preparing ourselves to stand against the enemy and his attacks. When we are asking God for a breakthrough, we are praying for heaven to invade earth. We are asking God to deliver us because we can't deliver ourselves. It's clear to us in those situations that only God can bring the breakthrough we need. If you've been praying for a while, I want to encourage you to keep going, keep asking, keep knocking, because God is listening. I've experienced so many times in my own life when I needed to hear from God.

A New Thing

When I was a college student, I went through a few months when life felt overwhelming. I'd gone to seminary because I thought God wanted me to be a missionary in India, but the more I prayed about that, the less sure I was. I remember thinking, *What if I'm not even supposed to be here? What if I got it all wrong and everyone else will graduate knowing where they're going and I won't have a clue?* As graduation day grew closer, every morning I would go for a walk in the woods near my dorm before classes began and would beg God to show me what to do. Each night I'd kneel by my bed in tears asking God for help. I felt like such a failure. I wanted to serve God with my whole life, but I didn't know what that would look like. Sometimes I'd think about my past, about where I'd come from, and wonder if that was what was wrong. Why would God choose someone whose father had committed suicide? Perhaps his death had been my fault after all. All the other students looked much more worthy to serve God than I did. I felt damaged. I prayed and I wept and I prayed.

One morning my reading for the day was from Isaiah 43:

> Remember not the former things,
>   nor consider the things of old.
> Behold, I am doing a new thing;
>   now it springs forth, do you not perceive it?
> I will make a way in the wilderness
>   and rivers in the desert. (vv. 18–19 ESV)

I thought it was a beautiful promise, but I didn't apply it to myself. In chapel that day, a professor preached from the same passage. I underlined it in my Bible and went off to my first class. As I knelt by my bed that evening,

I asked God one more time for a breakthrough. *Father, if You would just speak to me, whatever You want me to do, I'll do it. I just need to know that You're with me.* I was about to turn off my lamp when there was a gentle knock on my door. It was past lights out, and I knew that we weren't supposed to be in one another's rooms. I slipped out of bed and saw that an envelope had been pushed under my door. I picked it up and opened it. Inside was a message from one of my friends and a folded piece of paper. The note said that she'd been trying to track me down all day because God had given her a message for me. I unfolded the sheet of paper, and there in her beautiful calligraphy was the message from God:

> Remember not the former things,
>   nor consider the things of old.
> Behold, I am doing a new thing;
>   now it springs forth, do you not perceive it?
> I will make a way in the wilderness
>   and rivers in the desert. (Isa. 43:18–19 ESV)

It was a beautiful breakthrough. I still didn't know where I would go upon graduation, but I knew that God had a plan and that He was doing something new.

Sometimes when we pray for a breakthrough, it comes quickly, but sometimes we have to wait. God's Word is full of breakthroughs, but one of the most dramatic took place in the life of Daniel. We meet him in the Old Testament when things for God's chosen people were at their worst.

Daniel's Breakthrough

When Daniel was about fifteen years old, he was among the vast crowd of Israelites taken into captivity in Babylon. It was a catastrophic time. They had been warned over and over again through the prophets what would happen if they didn't repent and turn back to God, but they ignored every warning. Now Jerusalem and the temple had been destroyed and the people were living in a pagan land, ordered to bow down to pagan gods.

As Warren Wiersbe writes, "God would rather have His people living in shameful captivity in a pagan land than living like pagans in the Holy Land and disgracing His name."[1]

Daniel proved himself to be a godly man no matter where he lived. As he grew, he was given a place of honor in the palace, which did not sit well with others in authority. They were determined to get rid of him. King Darius loved and respected Daniel, but he was tricked into signing a decree that if anyone prayed to any god apart from the king for the next thirty days, they would be thrown into a lions' den. Those in high office knew that Daniel prayed to the Lord three times a day, and when they reported that Daniel had been seen praying, his fate was sealed.

What's deeply moving to me is that Daniel's prayers were never hidden. People knew that Daniel prayed to his God. His windows faced toward the ruins of Jerusalem, and three times a day he threw open those windows and got down on his knees to pray. Daniel also knew about the decree. He knew that continuing to pray put his life on the line. He prayed anyway. The king was distraught when those who hated Daniel reported that he had been caught praying, but he couldn't go back on a signed decree. In those days, a decree signed by a king was irrevocable. His last words to Daniel before he was taken off to be torn apart were these: "May your God, whom you serve so faithfully, rescue you" (Dan. 6:16).

If, like me, you heard the story of Daniel in the lions' den in Sunday school, your familiarity might blind you to the terror of this situation. History tells us that the Persians employed many forms of torture, some excruciatingly painful. They would have expected the lions to tear Daniel apart and that nothing would be left in the morning but a few bones.

So they threw him into the pit or cave, and the entrance was sealed with the king's royal seal so that no one could break it and rescue him. If anyone had ever needed a breakthrough, it was Daniel. I've often wondered what that night was like. We read that angels were sent to seal the mouths of the lions. That's a pretty spectacular breakthrough. In the morning, the king, who hadn't been able to sleep all night, hurried down to the den and called out before he had the heart to have the seal broken.

"Daniel, servant of the living God! Was your God, whom you serve so faith-fully, able to rescue you from the lions?"

Daniel answered, "Long live the king! My God sent his angel to shut the lions' mouths so that they would not hurt me, for I have been found innocent in his sight. And I have not wronged you, Your Majesty."

The king was overjoyed and ordered that Daniel be lifted from the den. Not a scratch was found on him, for he had trusted in his God. (Dan. 6:20–23)

The Bible contains many miraculous stories of deliverance. Here Daniel had an immediate answer, but sometimes, like you and me, he had to wait.

Delayed Breakthrough

Daniel is now eighty-five years old. The previous year fifty thousand Jews had been allowed to go back to Jerusalem to rebuild the temple. As part of the royal court, Daniel received regular updates and knew that things were not going well. The foundations of the temple had been laid, but there had been so much opposition (see Ezra 4) that everything had now stopped. Daniel was grieved that the work had stopped. What he didn't understand was that the sixteen-year delay was part of God's plan and the fulfillment of His promise to Jeremiah. Do you remember this well-loved verse?

"For I know the plans I have for you," says the LORD. "They are plans for good and not for disaster, to give you a future and a hope." (Jer. 29:11)

We love the hope of this verse, but this is what the verse before it says:

This is what the LORD says: "You will be in Babylon for seventy years. But then I will come and do for you all the good things I have promised, and I will bring you home again." (v. 10).

In his Old Testament commentary, Warren Wiersbe explains that the promise in Jeremiah was to the people of God and also to the temple of God. The first Jews were taken in 605 BC, and the first group returned in 536

BC, seventy years later. The temple was destroyed in 586 BC. When the fifty thousand returned in 536 BC, they began rebuilding but were immediately stopped. It would be sixteen years before they were able to start again, in 520, completing it in 515. God's timing is perfect, seventy years.[2] It took seventy years for the people to return and seventy years for the temple to be rebuilt. That may be more math than you need, but I want you to see the big picture for your life when God's timing seems to make no sense. God knows what He is doing. He is for you. He is with you. He has not forgotten you.

Daniel couldn't see the whole plan, and so he was grieved and was praying. This is actually where we get the Daniel Fast from.

> At that time I, Daniel, mourned for three weeks. I ate no choice food; no meat or wine touched my lips; and I used no lotions at all until the three weeks were over. (Dan. 10:2–3 NIV)

For three weeks, Daniel prayed for a breakthrough, and it seemed as if no breakthrough was coming. Then one day when Daniel was standing on the banks of the Tigris River, an angel appeared to him. I can't imagine what that sight must have been like, but it must have been magnificent, for Daniel, the one who had faced lions, fainted. The angel touched him and said this:

> Don't be afraid, Daniel. Since the first day you began to pray for understanding and to humble yourself before your God, your request has been heard in heaven. I have come in answer to your prayer. But for twenty-one days the spirit prince of the kingdom of Persia blocked my way. Then Michael, one of the archangels, came to help me, and I left him there with the spirit prince of the kingdom of Persia. (Dan. 10:12–13)

It's important to remember that when we are praying for a breakthrough, God sends His holy ambassadors to do battle for us.

> Are not all angels ministering spirits sent to serve those who will inherit salvation? (Heb. 1:14 NIV)

No Breakthrough

God's answer to Daniel's situation with the lions was an immediate break-through. You may have experienced an immediate breakthrough in your own life. But sometimes we don't get a breakthrough. Families pray fervently, gather prayer warriors, and don't get the answer they long for. In those heartbreaking times, we hold on to the goodness of God even when we don't understand the ways of God. If you have been there, I want you to know that the outcome had nothing to do with how you prayed, how often you prayed, how desperately you prayed. One day when you see Jesus face-to-face, all the questions will be gone. Until then, don't allow the enemy or any "well-meaning" friend to suggest that somehow you failed. God has a plan that is bigger than our understanding, and He has promised to bring good from everything that happens to us. This doesn't mean that everything is good or feels good, but He will bring good to those who love Him. God has a unique purpose for our lives and the lives of those we love.

> And we know that God causes everything to work together for the good of those who love God and are called according to his purpose for them. (Rom. 8:28)

Sometimes a breakthrough comes quickly, sometimes it's delayed, and sometimes we don't see the breakthrough we ask for at all. I wonder in those dark times if the breakthrough God is looking for is a breakthrough in us. Perhaps that is the most significant breakthrough of all. I think of Moses. Ever since the children of Israel had been delivered from slavery in Egypt, they had done nothing but complain. While Moses was receiving the Ten Commandments, the people were partying below, making idols out of gold. God was done with them.

> The LORD said to Moses, "Get going, you and the people you brought up from the land of Egypt. Go up to the land I swore to give to Abraham, Isaac, and Jacob. I told them, 'I will give this land to your descendants.' ... Go up to this land that flows with milk and honey. But I will not travel among you, for you are a stubborn and rebellious people." (Exod. 33:1, 3)

How would Moses and the people respond to this offer from God? Think about it. God was promising that they could have all the things they wanted. They could have the land He had promised to Abraham, the land flowing with milk and honey. There was just one catch. God wouldn't be going with them. How would you answer? If God said to you, "I'll answer every single prayer, give you the child, the husband, the career you've asked for. The only difference is that My presence won't be with you," how would you respond? My prayer is that we would respond as Moses did.

> Then Moses said, "If you don't personally go with us, don't make us leave this place." (Exod. 33:15)

I love his response. He's saying, "I'd rather wander around in the wilderness forever with You than move on without You." That's my response too. Everything without God is nothing. Nothing with God is everything. When we finally come to that place, what freedom, what victory! That is a spiritual breakthrough.

Who Are You?

Daniel and Moses were able to stand strong when everything around them was falling apart because they knew who they were—not their job assignments but their true identity. Although Daniel lived and worked in the palace of the king, he knew that he belonged to God, and nothing and no one could change his allegiance. Moses had experienced life in the palace and life on the run, and the rock he now stood on was the great I AM. So too for you and me. Because our identity is based on who we are in Christ, we can stand strong and pray and believe that God will bring a breakthrough no matter how long it takes, even if it's not what we expected. Understanding our true, eternal identity is huge; it changes everything.

For many years, I had no idea who I was, and when the pressure of life was overwhelming, I fell apart. Falling apart was the breakthrough I needed. Falling apart was God's gift to me. God began to strip away every layer or

161

mask that I depended on. I was no longer a contemporary Christian artist or a television host. I was a psychiatric patient diagnosed with a mental illness. I seriously considered ending my life because I didn't think I had any life left. What I discovered in my brokenness was heartbreakingly beautiful, a relationship with Jesus based on nothing I brought to the table but on who He is and how He loves. It didn't matter if I ever stood on a platform again. I knew who I was. I am Sheila Walsh, daughter of the King of Kings. That's who we are as God's daughters, and on days when it feels as if our identity is being shaken, we can call the following truths to mind.

I am chosen.

> You didn't choose me. I chose you. (John 15:16)

I am free.

> And you will know the truth, and the truth will set you free. (John 8:32)

I am a new person.

> This means that anyone who belongs to Christ has become a new person. (2 Cor. 5:17)

I am forgiven.

> He is so rich in kindness and grace that he purchased our freedom with the blood of his Son and forgave our sins. (Eph. 1:7)

I am not condemned.

> So now there is no condemnation for those who belong to Christ Jesus. (Rom. 8:1)

I am healed.

> By his wounds you are healed. (1 Pet. 2:24)

Finding our identity in anything other than Christ is like building our house on the edge of a volcano, and it could blow at any minute. If someone or something destroys that identity, we don't know who we are anymore. We were created to worship, and we will worship something whether it's our children, our image, our football team, or even our service to Christ. The bottom line remains: we were made for God, and nothing and no one else can fill the deep places in our souls. Even if you have a great marriage, a fulfilling career, and beautiful children, have you ever noticed that even on the best days there's still an ache?

If your identity is being a good mom and one of your kids goes off the rails, who are you then? If your identity is based on your job and you lose your job or you don't get that promotion, how do you repair the damage to your soul? If your identity is in being married and your husband leaves you for a younger woman, what does that do to who you think you are? If your identity is based on how you look, as you start to age, you will increasingly face challenges to that identity. There is no fountain of youth. Yes, there's Botox and plastic surgery and hair dye and makeup, but even if you can afford all that stuff, you can only do so much for so long.

If it's your honest prayer to have a real spiritual breakthrough in your life, a new level in prayer, a new authority in Christ, then you must begin to build your confidence not on who you are but on who our God is.

When our identity is in anything other than who we are in Christ, we will end up on shaky ground. We were made for so much more. If it's your honest prayer to have a real spiritual breakthrough in your life, a new level in prayer, a new authority in Christ, then you must begin to build your confidence not on who you are but on who our God is.

I wonder even as you've read this far if you're thinking, *This is all great, but it's a bit much right now.* You're up to your eyes in laundry, dishes in the sink, bills to be paid, and a breakthrough is the last thing on your mind. I understand that too. What I want you to know, however, is that God wants to be a part of all that, the little stuff, the daily stuff. He sees everything that concerns you, and He wants to be everything you need. For that to happen, you need to know who He is. There are so many verses in the Bible that tell us about His character. You might know that He is your shelter, but did you know that He is also a wonderful Counselor, that He will be your Father forever? You might take comfort in the truth that He is your peace, but did you know that He is also your strength? The Bible contains countless expressions of who God is. While you are praying, call out these Scripture passages but personalize them.

> He will be called:
> Wonderful Counselor, Mighty God,
>> Everlasting Father, Prince of Peace. (Isa. 9:6)

You are my wonderful Counselor. You are my mighty God. You are my everlasting Father. You are my Prince of Peace.

Make the truths of the Bible yours. Call them out. Declare them over your life!

> I love you, Lord;
>> you are my strength. (Ps. 18:1)

God is love, and all who live in love live in God, and God lives in them. And as we live in God, our love grows more perfect. (1 John 4:16–17)

> For you are my hiding place;
>> you protect me from trouble.
>> You surround me with songs of victory. (Ps. 32:7)

I am the Lord, and I do not change. (Mal. 3:6)

> The Lord is merciful and compassionate,
>> slow to get angry and filled with unfailing love. (Ps. 145:8)

There are so many more expressions of who God is. Ultimately, He is good, He is love, and He wants the best for you. If you are praying for a breakthrough in some area of your life, don't lose heart and don't give up. The enemy would love for you to quit before your answer comes, but press on for your breakthrough and remember this:

The one who is in you is greater than the one who is in the world. (1 John 4:4 NIV)

Praying women know that the greatest breakthrough is in their own hearts.

PRAYER REMINDERS

1. Pray believing that in every place where you need a breakthrough, God is at work.
2. As you pray, remember who God says you are.
3. Pray boldly, knowing that God's timing is perfect.

A PRAYER WHEN YOU NEED A BREAKTHROUGH

Father,

Thank You that You are a faithful God who listens to my prayers. I bring before You now every area in my life where I need a breakthrough: my family, my finances, my health. Help me spiritually, mentally, physically, emotionally. I ask for a breakthrough in Jesus's name! Amen.

TEN

Pray from a Place of Victory

Praying women know that
the battle is already won.

The pressing need in an age like our own, when so many people are praying so much, is not for greater activity but for greater authority.

Peter Grieg

When you were stuck in your old sin-dead life, you were incapable of responding to God. God brought you alive—right along with Christ! Think of it! All sins forgiven, the slate wiped clean, that old arrest warrant canceled and nailed to Christ's cross. He stripped all the spiritual tyrants in the universe of their sham authority at the Cross and marched them naked through the streets.

Colossians 2:13–15, The Message

Sometimes God drops the beginning of a new dream or vision into your heart like one single drop of rain, but you can tell there is more on the way. That is what happened to me two years ago, and now the rain is beginning to fall.

"I think we should see if the website domain name Praying Women is available," Barry said one morning over breakfast.

"What made you think of that?" I asked.

"I'm not sure, but I woke up at 3:00 a.m. with it on my mind," he said. "It wouldn't shift. I believe we're supposed to do something with this."

The idea of praying women struck a chord deep inside me. For the last three years, I had been studying prayer in my own life, but I had never thought about writing about it. It felt like such a huge subject to address. We decided to see if the website domain name was available. It was, but it was quite expensive. So we committed to wait and pray about buying it for a few days. Soon we both had such a strong sense that God had put this on our hearts, so we went ahead and purchased and registered the name.

"Now what?" Barry asked.

"I have no idea," I said. "I guess we just wait." So we waited.

A few weeks later, I got an email from a woman I'd never met before. She told me that she had been asked to invite twenty female Christian leaders from across America to an important meeting in Washington, DC, and wanted to know if I was available. I told her I'd check my calendar and get back to her. By the time I did, things had changed. "I can invite only four women now," she said. "Will you be one of them?" I said yes. Since we didn't know one another, we decided to meet for breakfast before we went into the main meeting. My flight into Washington was delayed, so I was a few minutes late. When I arrived, the other women were already deep in conversation. I introduced myself and sat down.

"We're talking about prayer," one of them said. "We even looked at getting the website Praying Women, but it's been taken."

I smiled and said, "Yes, by me."

It was clear to us right away that we had been gathered there that morning by God. We were all from very different walks of life. The youngest among us is a sharp lawyer who works in the foster care system. Another woman works with students across America, another with orphans in Africa, and another in a women's ministry in a large church. Our normal lives wouldn't have brought us all together, but God did. I realized that day that the purpose of me being in Washington had nothing to do with the meeting we were about to attend but everything to do with these four women and a common burning call on our lives about prayer. We had no idea what our involvement together would look like, but we knew that God had caused our paths to cross for a purpose. We determined that the next step would be to touch base with one another once a week.

Our Battle Cry

We began slow and small. On Monday mornings, we joined together on a video call, prayed for one another, and asked God what He wanted us to do. Soon the vision began to clarify itself. We were called to rally women across the country to pray. Our vision was not about an event or any one person. It would just be about prayer. Someone suggested the name She Loves Out Loud, because love is not silent and neither should we be when it comes to talking about the love and mercy of God. It became crystal clear that prayer is the one thing that unites every one of us. We had no idea where God might take this vision but we knew that as God's daughters we could do something together. No matter where we live, whether we are rich or poor, strong or weak, we can pray as one.

If you're a college student, if you're retired, if you're in a hospital bed, if you're in the workplace, if you're nine, if you're ninety-nine, we can join with others and pray.

I asked God to give us a verse that would be our theme verse, and I was drawn to Psalm 68:11:

> The Lord gave the command;
> a great company of women
> brought the good news. (HCSB)

Soon twelve of us were committed to the same vision and met every Monday on a video call. I have production meetings on Mondays at the studio where I work, so I'd join the call in work clothes and a little makeup, one of the California girls would join in her pajamas with her hair pulled up in a banana clip, a couple women would join in their cars as they drove to work. We were an interesting-looking group. Don't you love that God often chooses the least likely people for special assignments? I'm so glad we were very different. Different denominations, different skin colors, different life experiences, different ages but united by one thing: we love Jesus and believe that prayer changes things.

Our Monday morning calls were good, but we felt it was important to get together in one place to talk and to pray. So we met in the spring of 2019 at a ranch in East Texas. Over dinner the first night, we shared our stories of the ways that God had met each one of us in the broken spaces of life. I knew a few of the women by name or reputation, but I'd never heard their personal stories. The experience was profoundly moving, and one thing was clear: Jesus was the hero of every story. One had gone through an unwanted divorce, one had endured abuse, a couple of us had struggled with depression, but the common theme was that at the lowest point in our lives, we had discovered who we are and whose we are, and doing so had made us brave; not only brave but victorious in Christ. We had learned to overcome in His name. The very things the enemy intended to use to break us in Christ's hands had made us stronger. It became clear to me why God had put a passion for prayer on each one of our hearts. Together we had tasted the bitter side of life—injustice, betrayal, cancer, mental illness, suicide in our families. We didn't just believe that our God is a Healer, a Redeemer, a Restorer, a Deliverer, a Shelter, an Advocate, a Strong Tower. We knew He is because He has been that for each of us. Now we were ready to fight for our sisters.

On the second day, we moved outside to pray. We knelt in a circle and placed our hands on the soil. Some of us lay flat on our faces, and we worshiped and prayed. We prayed for our nation, for those who have lost hope, for those who have been battered by life, for those who feel lost, unloved, unseen. I thought of all the tears that had fallen on the soil in previous generations, of prayers watered by tears asking God for revival. We asked God if we could be the ones who lived to see the fruit of those tears and faith-filled prayers. J. Edwin Orr once said that "every revival in history could be traced to find at its source a group of people gathered for prayer."[1] Our history records a time when that happened at Yale University.

> At Yale University in 1905, prayer meetings began to multiply. A faculty member was so impressed that he sent John R. Mott a letter in which he wrote: "We want you to come to Yale for a series of meetings. . . . The Spirit of God is here with us in power. . . . I have never known a time when there were so many inquirers." The result of those meetings was an awakening in which one third of the Yale student body were involved in small group Bible Studies. K. S. LaTourette goes on to write that the class of 1909, who were freshmen in 1905, produced more missionaries than any other class in the history of Yale.[2]

I long to see a revival like that again on college campuses, in towns and cities across the nation.

In conversation around the dying flames of a fire that evening, we each shared our battle verses. We discovered that each one of us had made a Scripture passage our own, our personal dagger from the Word of God for the fiercest battles of our lives. This is mine:

> I remain confident of this:
>> I will see the goodness of the LORD
>> in the land of the living.
> Wait for the LORD;
>> be strong and take heart
>> and wait for the LORD. (Ps. 27:13–14 NIV)

When I was hospitalized with severe clinical depression, the overwhelming temptation was to take my own life. The enemy would whisper to me in the darkest hours of the night:

You're just like your father.
You won't make it out of here alive.
Just end it now.

No one will ever trust you again.

You are all alone.

You will never win this battle.

In tears, I would literally drag myself out of bed, raise my arms high, and pray this passage out loud over and over:

> I remain confident of this:
> I will see the goodness of the LORD
> in the land of the living.
> Wait for the LORD;
> be strong and take heart
> and wait for the LORD.

Honestly, it didn't *feel* true. I didn't feel that I would ever see the goodness of the Lord again in the land of the living. I knew I would see His goodness when my life down here was over, but I didn't know how I would ever overcome the darkness on this earth. If you have ever experienced severe depression, you know the desperate hopelessness and darkness, as if your soul is trapped in a perpetual winter.

Although I didn't feel those words were true, I declared them to be true. One night I declared it so loudly that two of the other patients and a nurse came to make sure I wasn't seeing things in my room! Psalm 27:13–14 became my fighting verses. Do you have a fighting verse? Is there a Scripture passage that you hold on to, that you declare over your life when everything around you seems to be falling apart? If you don't have such a passage, consider using one of my favorites.

> The name of the LORD is a strong fortress;
> the godly run to him and are safe. (Prov. 18:10)

> Those who live in the shelter of the Most High
> will find rest in the shadow of the Almighty.
> This I declare about the LORD:

He alone is my refuge, my place of safety;
  he is my God, and I trust him. (Ps. 91:1–2)

The LORD is good,
  a strong refuge when trouble comes.
  He is close to those who trust in him. (Nah. 1:7)

But you are a tower of refuge to the poor, O LORD,
  a tower of refuge to the needy in distress.
You are a refuge from the storm
  and a shelter from the heat. (Isa. 25:4)

We can declare and rest in these verses with absolute confidence because they are the Word of God. We don't just hope they are true; we know they are true. The smallest, weakest person who places her trust in Christ against all odds makes the demons in hell tremble.

Prayer, Christ's Weapon of Choice

Have you ever noticed how many times in the Gospels we read that Christ withdrew to pray?

After sending them home, he went up into the hills by himself to pray. (Matt. 14:23)

Before daybreak the next morning, Jesus got up and went out to an isolated place to pray. (Mark 1:35)

One day soon afterward Jesus went up on a mountain to pray, and he prayed to God all night. (Luke 6:12)

There are many more references to Christ praying, all night long, before daybreak, in Gethsemane before He faced the greatest battle of all. Prayer was Christ's weapon of choice on this earth, but did you know that it's been His weapon ever since?

There were many priests under the old system, for death prevented them from remaining in office. But because Jesus lives forever, his priesthood lasts forever. Therefore he is able, once and forever, to save those who come to God through him. He lives forever to intercede with God on their behalf. (Heb. 7:23–25)

Will you pause for a moment and let that sink in? Christ, the spotless Lamb of God, the One whose words brought our world into being, the One who holds the stars and planets in place, the One who was betrayed, beaten, tortured, and crucified, the One who rose from the dead is praying for you right now!

In the above text, the writer to the Hebrews talks about the old system in which a high priest once a year entered the Holy of Holies to make a sacrifice to cover the sins of the people. It was an imperfect system. The priests were human. They would die, and then a replacement would have to be found. Our High Priest is Jesus, who died once and rose again. There will never be any interruption in His prayers for us. Prayer is not only Christ's weapon of choice but also God's chosen fragrance in heaven.

The Fragrance of Heaven

Our son, Christian, is a student at Texas A & M in College Station, Texas. When he left for college, we sold our house and downsized. We used to live in Frisco, Texas, but now we're in Dallas, thirty minutes closer to College Station. So far, Christian doesn't seem to have noticed that we are gradually inching toward him.

When we visit him, we love to stay in a particular hotel for a few reasons. The hotel has a train theme. College Station was so named because it used to be the stop where students would get off the train to go to college. In the elevator, you don't press a button for your floor but for your platform. The hotel's mascot is a sheep, and there is a life-sized "flock" scattered around the hotel. The first time we stayed there Barry thought it would be funny to fetch one of the sheep from the lobby after I was asleep and put it next to me. If you happened to be staying there at that time, I would like to apologize if you woke to a blood-curdling scream.

But the main reason we love this hotel is because the moment you walk through the doors, its signature fragrance greets you. It's not like anything I've smelled before, and the fragrance is everywhere—in the lobby, the elevator, and the rooms. We asked about it one time, and a staff member told us it's oak and ember, a woodsy smell reminiscent of Texas nights and specifically chosen to be used in that hotel alone.

God has specifically chosen one fragrance for heaven, and it's the prayers of His people.

In the Revelation that was given to John on the island of Patmos, John wrote this speaking of Jesus:

> He stepped forward and took the scroll from the right hand of the one sitting on the throne. And when he took the scroll, the four living beings and the twenty-four elders fell down before the Lamb. Each one had a harp, and they held gold bowls filled with incense, which are the prayers of God's people. (Rev. 5:7–8)

Again, in Revelation, John wrote:

> Then another angel with a gold incense burner came and stood at the altar. And a great amount of incense was given to him to mix with the prayers of God's people as an offering on the gold altar before the throne. The smoke of the incense, mixed with the prayers of God's holy people, ascended up to God from the altar where the angel had poured them out. (8:3–4)

The psalmist David knew that our prayers are like a fragrant offering to God.

> Accept my prayer as incense offered to you,
>   and my upraised hands as an evening offering. (Ps. 141:2)

God could have chosen anything as the fragrance of heaven. He could have chosen church attendance or tithing or good behavior. He chose prayer. When this present life is over and we finally enter heaven, there it will be, that familiar fragrance, the prayers of God's people.

Sometimes our prayers are offerings of worship, sometimes of petition, but there are times when our prayers need to be prayers of authority, boldly prayed in the name of Jesus. We can pray with confident authority because of what Christ has done for us.

Time to Take Your Seat

On June 6, 2019, the world paused to honor a significant date, the seventy-fifth anniversary of D-day. On that day in 1944, which was the beginning of the end of the Second World War, British, American, and Canadian forces invaded northern France by means of beach landings in Normandy. Their steely commitment was to push back Hitler's Nazi war machine. I remember as a child asking my mum what she remembered of the war. She told me about the evening a young German paratrooper who had missed his landing spot came down in my grandparents' back garden. My grandfather called for the Home Guard to come and take him away, but before they arrived, Mum slipped out to take a look at this "enemy" soldier. "He was just a boy," she said. "How could this be the enemy?"

Today we face a war, however, in which the enemy is very clear. There can be no missing his motives or evil intent, no negotiating, no possibility of a peace treaty because he is pure evil. But we can defeat him when we pray with authority. To do so, we must notice where we are sitting, and that begins by understanding where Christ is sitting right now.

> I also pray that you will understand the incredible greatness of God's power for us who believe him. This is the same mighty power that raised Christ from the dead and seated him in the place of honor at God's right hand in the heavenly realms. Now he is far above any ruler or authority or power or leader or anything else—not only in this world but also in the world to come.

God has put all things under the authority of Christ and has made him head over all things for the benefit of the church. (Eph. 1:19–22)

Jesus is seated at God's right hand. Paul goes on to explain that because of where Jesus is, we have been given a significant upgrade in where we are.

But God is so rich in mercy, and he loved us so much, that even though we were dead because of our sins, he gave us life when he raised Christ from the dead. (It is only by God's grace that you have been saved!) For he raised us from the dead along with Christ and seated us with him in the heavenly realms because we are united with Christ Jesus. (2:4–6)

Frankly, this is a bit difficult to understand. What does it mean that we've been seated in heavenly realms? Right now, as far as I can see, I'm seated at my desk in Dallas. So what is Paul saying? A few things. One thing for sure: just as death and judgment are behind Christ, they are behind us too. Death has no power over a believer. We don't ever have to be afraid. We will go straight from this life to be with Jesus. Also, we will not face God's judgment at the great white throne. That is only for those who have never accepted Christ's sacrifice for their sins. We will, however, stand before Christ to be judged.

For we must all appear before the judgment seat of Christ, so that each of us may receive what is due us for the things done while in the body, whether good or bad. (2 Cor. 5:10 NIV)

That judgment, you'll notice, is not about punishment but about rewards. Don't think for a moment that God misses everything you do to serve Him. Whether anyone else sees or not, God does. Many people, myself included, have been gifted with public ministries, but don't think that these are more significant to God. I have a friend who isn't able to leave her house, but she devotes a great deal of her day to prayer. I've met many women in the poorest parts of Africa who quietly serve God every day. My big sister, Frances, has a lovely voice. She serves God quietly in places where there's no big audience or applause. I stand on very big stages all over the world, but I often say to her, "When we get to heaven, will you say hello to Jesus from me? I think you'll be closer!" Whatever you do for God might not be applauded much down here, but just wait until you get home!

So death and judgment are behind us, but what else is Paul saying?

A Change of Address

We get a little more clarity when we read this:

> Since, then, you have been raised with Christ, set your hearts on things above, where Christ is, seated at the right hand of God. Set your minds on things above, not on earthly things. For you died, and your life is now hidden with Christ in God. (Col. 3:1–3 NIV)

When God sees us, He sees us seated with Christ already. It's a done deal.

Paul's encouragement to the Colossians is helping them see that, yes, you may be here for a while longer, but this is not your real home. It's not our real home either. He's encouraging us to set our hearts and our minds on what is going to last forever. Every decision you face, every day before you set out, remember who you are. It will change how you live.

If you were invited to Buckingham Palace to meet Queen Elizabeth, how would you prepare? I'm sure you'd buy a nice outfit and perhaps a fancy hat. I had the privilege of meeting the royal family once at Holyrood Palace in Edinburgh. It was a wonderful experience, but it was over in a moment. I love Queen Elizabeth, but she is a human monarch.

You and I are children of the King of Kings. We're not invited into His presence for a moment; we get to stay forever. That makes me want to live differently now. I pray it does the same for you too. I'm asking God that you will be able to hold your head up high no matter what. No matter who has tried to diminish you, disrespect you, leave you, those things have a shelf life, a sell-by date. You have a future in heaven that no one can touch. You are a loved child of God.

All Rise

There is a very moving scene in the British television series *Victoria*. Victoria was very young, only eighteen, when she became queen. One of her palace advisors told her that on her coronation day, the "Hallelujah Chorus" from Handel's *Messiah* would be played. He explained that as was tradition, everyone else would stand, but because she will have just been crowned queen, she should remain seated. The coronation was a magnificent event, and as the first notes of the "Hallelujah Chorus" were struck by an eighty-piece orchestra and 157 singers, the entire assembled crowd in Westminster Abbey rose to their feet, as did the eighteen-year-old newly crowned queen of England. It's a true story and a tribute to a young queen who recognized One greater than she. What else could she do but stand?

> Hallelujah! Hallelujah! Hallelujah!
> Hallelujah! Hallelujah! Hallelujah!
> Hallelujah! Hallelujah! Hallelujah!
> For the Lord God omnipotent reigneth.
> Hallelujah! Hallelujah! Hallelujah! Hallelujah!
> Hallelujah! Hallelujah! Hallelujah! Hallelujah!
>
> The kingdom of this world
> Is become the kingdom of our Lord,
> And of His Christ, and of His Christ;
> And He shall reign for ever and ever,
> And He shall reign for ever and ever,
> For ever and ever, forever and ever.
>
> King of Kings, and Lord of Lords,
> King of Kings, and Lord of Lords,
> King of Kings, and Lord of Lords,
> And Lord of Lords.
>
> And He shall reign forever and ever,
> King of Kings! And Lord of Lords!
> And He shall reign forever and ever,
> King of Kings! And Lord of Lords!

Hallelujah! Hallelujah! Hallelujah! Hallelujah!
Hallelujah!

What's in a Name?

Understanding what it means to be seated with Christ changes how we pray. Because we are *in Christ* and we pray *in His name*, we pray with the authority of that name. If we could truly grasp the weight of the authority of the name of Christ not only would it change how we pray, but it would also change us. When Christ saw that kind of understanding not in a Jewish believer but in a Roman soldier, he was astonished.

> When Jesus returned to Capernaum, a Roman officer came and pleaded with him, "Lord, my young servant lies in bed, paralyzed and in terrible pain."
>
> Jesus said, "I will come and heal him."
>
> But the officer said, "Lord, I am not worthy to have you come into my home. Just say the word from where you are, and my servant will be healed. I know this because I am under the authority of my superior officers, and I have authority over my soldiers. I only need to say, 'Go,' and they go, or 'Come,' and they come. And if I say to my slaves, 'Do this,' they do it."
>
> When Jesus heard this, he was amazed. Turning to those who were following him, he said, "I tell you the truth, I haven't seen faith like this in all Israel!" . . .
>
> Then Jesus said to the Roman officer, "Go back home. Because you believed, it has happened." And the young servant was healed that same hour. (Matt. 8:5–10, 13)

This Roman officer, in charge of about one hundred soldiers, was obviously a man of faith, and he understood authority. He was clearly a compassionate man, seeking out Jesus because a young servant of his was sick. He knew there is power in the name of the Lord: "Just say the word." When Christ triumphed over death and the grave, there was a mighty power shift. As we saw at the beginning of this chapter, the Message translation puts it this way:

He stripped all the spiritual tyrants in the universe of their sham authority at the Cross and marched them naked through the streets. (Col. 2:15)

Another translation says this:

He canceled the record of the charges against us and took it away by nailing it to the cross. In this way, he disarmed the spiritual rulers and authorities. He shamed them publicly by his victory over them on the cross. (NIV)

Because of Jesus, we win. We live in a culture that increasingly dishonors God, that tries to throw God out of schools and mocks Him on television or in movies, but this won't last forever. One of my favorite passages of Scripture, the great christological hymn of Philippians 2, reminds us of a day that's coming. Speaking of Jesus, Paul wrote:

> Though he was God,
>   he did not think of equality with God
>   as something to cling to.
> Instead, he gave up his divine privileges;
>   he took the humble position of a slave
>   and was born as a human being.
> When he appeared in human form,
>   he humbled himself in obedience to God
>   and died a criminal's death on a cross.
> Therefore, God elevated him to the place of highest honor
>   and gave him the name above all other names,
> that at the name of Jesus every knee should bow,
>   in heaven and on earth and under the earth,
> and every tongue declare that Jesus Christ is Lord,
>   to the glory of God the Father. (vv. 6–11)

I once asked a friend's child, "What does it mean to pray 'in Jesus's name'?"

He replied, "It means we can open our eyes now."

I loved his answer, but in reality, praying in Jesus's name means way more than an announcement that the prayer is over. It means we come in His righteousness. It means we pray with His authority. It means we pray with His power. That is such good news because, if you're like me, you'll have good days and bad days. There are days when I get up early, meet with God, worship along with the playlist in my car . . . and then there are those other days. You know what those days look like. I'm guessing most of us have them.

The reality of praying in the name of Jesus is that we are welcomed because of everything Jesus did right, not anything we did right or wrong. We have an all-access pass into the throne room of God because of Jesus. We come in His name. We are welcomed in His name. We pray in His name. We have victory in His name.

Praying women know that the battle is already won.

PRAYER REMINDERS

1. Pray, remembering that prayer is Christ's weapon of choice.
2. Pray, knowing that you are adding to the fragrance of heaven.
3. Pray in the authority of the powerful name of Jesus.

A PRAYER WHEN YOU'RE PRAYING FROM A PLACE OF VICTORY

Father,

I come boldly to the throne of grace and mercy in the name of Jesus. I know that I have no goodness of my own, but I thank You that I'm covered by the blood of Jesus. I thank You that I can bring all my requests before You in His name. I thank You that I am welcomed in His name. I thank You that I can pray for my family with authority in Jesus's name. I thank You that I can bring every concern I have to You in Jesus's name. Thank You that when You look at me, You don't see my sin; You see His sacrifice. Thank You for the beautiful, wonderful, powerful name of Jesus. Amen.

Conclusion

I began this book by saying that God is not looking for perfect words or perfect people—He longs for our ongoing daily presence in prayer and worship. I understand that now at a depth I never have before. I'll never be perfect, but I love that I'm welcomed into the presence of God just as I am. And although the wonder of this is hard to grasp, I know He loves my presence too. I pray that you know this truth as well. Even now I'm praying for you. I'm asking God to communicate to you in ways where my words fail how much He loves you, just as you are right now. You are not welcomed more on your best days or welcomed less when you feel that you've blown it. He waits with open arms for you every day. That image makes me smile and takes me right back to the summer I turned eighteen.

The summer before I went off to college, I volunteered at a drop-in center for senior citizens. I helped prepare and serve lunches and afternoon teas. I played dominoes and card games and listened to countless stories about what our little seaside town used to be like in what they called "better days." I laughed at bad jokes and told my share of them too. They were a loud and happy crowd, but there was one gentleman who always sat in the corner, alone. He wouldn't talk or come to the table for lunch, so after we'd served those at the dining table, I would take his lunch to him on a tray.

One day I decided to pull up a chair beside him and just sit there as he ate. He gave me a dismissive look and carried on eating. I sat there every day after that. I just sat there quietly as he ate—not so quietly. On day ten, he spoke. "I'm an American!" he announced.

"That's awesome," I said. "I hope to visit there one day."

He turned to me with what looked like hope in his eyes and said, "If you ever get to Poughkeepsie, will you tell them George said hi?"

I promised him that I would, though I had no idea what a "Poughkeepsie" was. Was it a family, a place? I had no clue but made a mental note to find out.

Now that George had entrusted me with this sacred mission, he opened up and began to have his lunch at the table every day on two conditions: that he would have his meal served last and that I would sit with him.

What has stayed in my mind all these years is how this quiet, lonely man transformed into the one who cried out every day as I walked through the Ayrshire Senior Center doors, "You came!" The pure joy that came to his face touched my heart so deeply. And the first time I landed in Poughkeepsie, which is in New York, by the way, I shouted as loudly as I could, "George says hi!"

The delight that came to George's face doesn't hold a candle to how God feels about you when you walk through the doors into His presence. I had to get on a bus each day and then walk a mile to get to the center, but you just have to say, "Hello, Father. I'm here." You don't have to wait until you feel as if you're in a better place; you can enter His presence when you're happy, sad, confused, angry, afraid, or whatever else you might be feeling.

Some days I wake with gratitude on my lips, others with an overwhelming sense of my need for Christ for the day that lies ahead. There are mornings when I wake simply in love with Jesus and those when His name on my lips is a cry for His presence. My days, like yours, are different, but the one thing that has become a constant for me is that whatever my cry is, it's to Jesus. This is prayer. At times, we'll kneel in reverent awe. At times, we'll stand with arms raised to heaven in praise and worship. There will be days when we are facedown on the carpet, tears streaming down our cheeks, and days when we'll dance in the rain telling Him how much we love Him. Prayer is being with Christ, aligning ourselves with the things

He cares about, battling in the spiritual realm for our family members and friends, and resting in His presence.

When I was a younger Christian, I had prayer firmly on my to-do list. It was something I could tick off like brush my teeth, walk the dog, make my bed. But not anymore. Now my closest companion in life is Christ. Let me explain what I mean by that in light of the significant relationships in my life, because this is important. Barry and I have been married for twenty-six years. We have been through serious ups and downs, but I love him more today than I did on that snowy December morning in 1994. Our son, Christian, is twenty-four. He has been an absolute joy to raise, and we share a very special bond. The day he was born, something in me was born too—the heart of a mother. I would lay down my life for my son. I am profoundly grateful too for my family, my close friends, and the work I get to do through Life Outreach International. All of these relationships give my life joy and rich meaning, but not one of them comes close to my relationship with Christ. The best of human relationships are flawed.

When Barry and I were first married, many of our arguments happened because I expected him to be everything I needed, whether I was able to articulate what I needed or not. I thought he should just *know*. When Christian went off to college, I cried for about a week. I was so proud of him and I trusted God in him, but suddenly he was out there on his own. I couldn't stay awake until I knew he was home or make sure he ate something before he headed off to class. He was off on his own great adventure. Some of my closest friends are in different places than they were a few years ago. We used to work together every weekend, and now they are on new, wonderful paths, and at times my heart aches because I miss how things used to be. But here's the good news: the constant in my life is Jesus. He is my closest companion, the love of my life. I talk to Him about everything. And you can too.

When I told Barry that I was thinking about joining Weight Watchers because I thought I could stand to lose ten pounds, he said innocently, "Is that all?" Instead of smacking him with a frozen fish, I said to Jesus, "Did you hear that?" and He did. When Christian decided to take up scuba diving and become certified as a deep-sea diver, I said to Jesus, "What if something goes wrong?" and He said, "I'll be there." When a friend makes new friends and I feel a bit left out, I tell Jesus, and He says, "I know, but I am always here."

What I'm trying to say is not that we should let our husbands off the hook when they say hurtful things, or stop being concerned about our children, or no longer grieve life's inevitable losses—not at all. What I'm saying is that we have One who is always with us, who always has time for us, who will never leave us. Christ cares about everything going on in your life right now, big and small. This is the gift to every praying woman.

So when we don't know what to say, we have His name, Jesus. We enter our Father's presence, believing that He is listening and waiting for us. We pray and we pray and we don't give up because Jesus is teaching us to be relentless. When life is hard, when the pain is real, we don't stop praying but instead press into His presence, knowing that Jesus, our High Priest, has been there and understands. On the days, the weeks, the months when God seems silent and nothing makes sense to us, we trust Him even though we don't always understand His ways. We use the Word of God as a prayer book for our daily lives, and we walk into every day fully suited up in the armor of God, with our daggers ready. We pray for a breakthrough, and we thank our Father that because of Jesus the battle is already won.

I pray that we meet one day, but until then, I pray this blessing over you, my sister:

And now to him who can keep you on your feet, standing tall in his bright presence, fresh and celebrating—to our one God, our only Savior, through Jesus Christ, our Master, be glory, majesty, strength, and rule before all time, and now, and to the end of all time. Yes. (Jude 24–25 Message)

We've come so far, and yet in many ways we're just beginning to understand the power of prayer. I'm excited to see what God will do as we move forward together. Remember, He is the God of the impossible!

Praying Women

1. Praying women know it's okay to start where they are.

2. Praying women believe that God is listening right now.

3. Praying women never stop praying until they receive God's answer.

4. Praying women press through in prayer even when life is tough.

5. Praying women pray through their heartache until it becomes their authority.

6. Praying women trust God in the silence and the not knowing.

7. Praying women don't depend on their own strength but on the power of God's Word.

8. Praying women put on the whole armor of God, trusting in His promises.

9. Praying women know that the greatest breakthrough is in their own hearts.

10. Praying women know that the battle is already won.

Acknowledgments

First of all, thank you to the entire Baker Publishing family. Dwight Baker, you and your team continue to uphold the rich heritage of Baker's commitment to building up the body of Christ through books. It's an honor to publish with you.

Thank you to my wonderful editor, Rebekah Guzman. I'm grateful for your vision, your hard and creative work, and your patience with my crazy schedule and the fact that I never remember how to do my endnotes!

Thank you to Mark Rice and Eileen Hanson. I love working closely with both of you, and when you fly into Dallas for dinner, that's the best. You make me laugh and you make me think, and you are so good at what you do.

Thank you to Dave Lewis and the entire amazing Baker sales team. You have such a gift for understanding the heart of a message and championing it.

Thank you to Brianna DeWitt and Olivia Peitsch. You are always looking for new ways to get the message out. I'm so grateful for you.

Thank you to Patti Brinks for your caring and creative artistic direction and your endless patience with me. You are a joy to work with.

Thank you to Meshali Mitchell. You are so much more than a photographer. You are an artist and a friend.

Thank you to my amazing literary agent, Shannon Marven, and the team at Dupree Miller. Shannon, you are one of the most gifted people I know. You lead with grace and vision.

Thank you to Caleb Peavy and Unmutable. I am grateful for your creativity and the level of excellence you bring to every project.

Thank you to James and Betty Robison for the joy of standing beside you to share God's love with a broken world through Life Today and Life Outreach International.

I want to thank my little dogs, Tink and Maggie, for sitting patiently at my feet month after month as I wrote and for the occasional much-needed lick.

To my husband, Barry, thank you seems inadequate to express my gratitude for the amount of time and creative energy you devoted to this book. You walked and prayed through every step with me, sitting up until midnight reading chapters out loud, making countless cups of tea. I love you and thank God for you every day.

To my son, Christian. Your FaceTime calls and texts to cheer me on meant so much. I love being your mum.

Finally to the One I will never find enough words to thank. To God my Father for loving me, to Christ my Savior for giving Your life for me, and to the Holy Spirit for Your comfort and guidance. I am Yours, forever.

Notes

Chapter 1 Pray When You Don't Know What to Say

1. Beliefnet, accessed June 29, 2019, https://www.beliefnet.com/quotes/evangelical
/c/corrie-ten-boom/is-prayer-your-steering-wheel-or-your-spare-tire.aspx.

Chapter 2 Pray Because God Is Waiting for You

1. William Barclay, *The Gospel of Luke* (Edinburgh, Scotland: St. Andrews Press, 1953), 224.
2. A. W. Tozer, *The Pursuit of God* (Chicago: Moody, 1961), 13.
3. http://gods-word-first.org/bible-study/613commandments.html.

Chapter 3 Pray . . . and Don't Give Up

1. William Rees, "Here Is Love Vast as the Ocean," Hymnary.org, accessed July 8, 2019, https://hymnary.org/text/here_is_love_vast_as_the_ocean.

Chapter 4 Pray Hardest When It's Hardest to Pray

1. William Barclay, *The Gospel of Mark*, rev. ed. (Louisville, KY: Westminster John Knox, 1975), 324.
2. Dan Hayes, "Prayer Is Valuable to God," Cru, accessed June 29, 2019, https://www.cru
.org/us/en/blog/spiritual-growth/prayer/seven-reasons-to-pray.7.html.
3. C. S. Lewis, *The Magician's Nephew*, The Chronicles of Narnia (New York: Harper-Collins, 1950), 86–87.

Chapter 5 Pray Through Your Pain

1. Christian Ellis, "'God's Almighty Kindness and Love': Joni Eareckson Tada Shares Good News after Hospital Scare," CBN News, April 12, 2019, https://www1.cbn.com/cbnne
ws/us/2019/april/gods-almighty-kindness-and-love-joni-eareckson-tada-shares-good-news
-after-hospital-scare.

Chapter 6 Pray When God Seems Silent

1. Rev. T. G. Ragland, quoted in William MacDonald's *Believer's Bible Commentary* (Nashville: Nelson, 1989), 1538

Chapter 7 Pray with the Power of the Word of God

1. William Shakespeare, *The Taming of the Shrew* (Oxford, UK: Oxford University Press, 1990), act 5, scene 2, lines 136–38.
2. Benjamin Kandt, "Augustine and the Psalms," PrayPsalms.org, August 28, 2017, https://praypsalms.org/saint-augustine-the-psalms-f2c7edf146d8.
3. Ambrose, "Delightful Book of the Psalms," Crossroads Initiative, posted June 15, 2017, https://www.crossroadsinitiative.com/media/articles/delightfulbookofthe psalms/.
4. Athanasius, "Praying the Psalms," The Prayer Foundation, posted 2001, http://www .prayerfoundation.org/athanasius_praying_the_psalms.htm.
5. Joni Eareckson Tada, "Speaking God's Language: How Scripture Can Add Power to Your Prayers," Redeemer Churches and Ministries, originally published in *Pray!* magazine, 2006, https://www.redeemer.com/learn/prayer/prayer_and_fasting/speaking_gods_language _how_scripture_can_add_power_to_your_prayers.
6. Walter Brueggemann, *Praying the Psalms* (Eugene, OR: Wipf & Stock, 2007), 1.
7. Eugene Peterson, *The Psalms as Tools for Prayer* (San Francisco: Harper & Row, 1989), 14.
8. Donald Whitney, *Praying the Bible* (Wheaton: Crossway, 2015), 46.
9. Dietrich Bonhoeffer, *Life Together* (New York: Harper & Row, 1954), 45–46.

Chapter 8 Pray with Your Armor On

1. C. S. Lewis, *The Screwtape Letters* (New York: Harper One, 1996), 16–17, Kindle.
2. Richard Foster, *Spiritual Classics* (New York: HarperCollins, 2000), 48.

Chapter 9 Pray When You Need a Breakthrough

1. Warren Wiersbe, *The Wiersbe Bible Commentary* OT (Colorado Springs: David C. Cook, 2017), 1344.
2. Wiersbe, *Wiersbe Bible Commentary* OT, 1381.

Chapter 10 Pray from a Place of Victory

1. Dan Hayes, "A Prerequisite to Spiritual Awakening," Cru, accessed June 29, 2019, https ://www.cru.org/us/en/blog/spiritual-growth/prayer/seven-reasons-to-pray.6.html.
2. Dan Hayes, "Prayer Is Valuable to God," Cru, accessed June 29, 2019, https://www.cru .org/us/en/blog/spiritual-growth/prayer/seven-reasons-to-pray.7.html.

Sheila Walsh grew up in Scotland and has spoken to over six million women around the world. Her passion is being a Bible teacher, making God's Word practical, and sharing her own story of how God met her when she was at her lowest point and lifted her up again.

Her message: GOD IS FOR YOU!

Sheila loves writing and has sold more than five million books. She is also the cohost of the television program *Life Today*, airing in the US, Canada, Europe, and Australia with over one hundred million viewers daily.

Calling Texas home, Sheila lives in Dallas with her husband, Barry; her son, Christian; and two little dogs, Tink and Maggie, who rule the roost.

You can stay in touch with her on Facebook at sheilawalshconnects, on Twitter @sheilawalsh, and on Instagram at @sheilawalsh1.

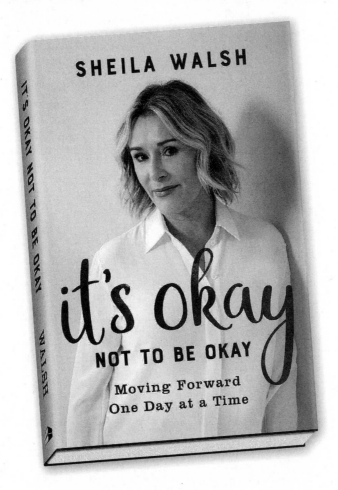

Connect with Sheila

To subscribe to her **newsletter**, read her **blog**, and learn more about Sheila's speaking, visit

SheilaWalsh.com

Additional Resources from Sheila